LIFE INSURANCE INVESTING 101

A Beginner's Guide to Guaranteed Income for Life

Usiere Uko

ISBN-13: 979-8-253-41236-7

SECOND EDITION

...To new frontiers, learning and growing

CONTENTS

INTRODUCTION

SIMPLE STRATEGIES FOR GROWING WEALTH AS A BEGINNER

In today's financial landscape, individuals are constantly searching for innovative ways to create wealth and secure their financial future. One tool that often goes overlooked is life insurance. While many view life insurance primarily as a safety net for loved ones, it can also be a powerful asset that helps you generate income and build wealth.

Life Insurance Investing 101: Simple Strategies for Growing Wealth with Life Insurance aims to change the way you think about life insurance by revealing its potential as a lucrative financial resource.

This book is designed for anyone who is curious about life insurance, whether you're a complete novice or someone who has been contemplating the benefits of policies for some time. We'll take you through the basics, demystifying complex terms and concepts in straightforward language. You'll learn about the different types of life insurance policies, how cash value accumulates, and the role dividends can play in your financial strategy.

Throughout the chapters, we'll explore practical methods for accessing your policy's cash value and generating income through various avenues, including loans and investments. We'll also highlight the common pitfalls to avoid, ensuring that you make informed decisions that align with your financial goals.

By the end of this book, you'll have a clear understanding of how to leverage your life insurance policy as a valuable asset. Get ready to transform your approach to financial planning and discover the wealth-building potential that life insurance can offer. Let's embark on this journey together and unlock the power of life insurance for your financial future

PART 1: WHY LIFE INSURANCE?

1: WHAT IS LIFE INSURANCE?

UNDERSTANDING LIFE INSURANCE AS A FINANCIAL TOOL

Life insurance is a financial product designed to provide a safety net for your loved ones in the event of your passing. At its core, life insurance is an agreement between you and an insurance company where, in exchange for regular payments, or premiums, the insurer promises to pay a specified sum of money to your designated beneficiaries when you pass away.

This payout, known as the death benefit, is often used to cover funeral expenses, replace lost income, or support dependents financially in the absence of the policyholder.

KEY CONCEPTS OF LIFE INSURANCE

Life insurance serves two main purposes: protection and, in certain cases, wealth-building. The traditional role of life insurance is to provide financial support to families during difficult times. However, certain types of life insurance go beyond providing a death benefit; they also have a savings or investment component that grows over time.

This is known as the "cash value" component, and it's what makes certain life insurance policies suitable for wealth-building and income generation.

WHY LIFE INSURANCE MATTERS

For beginners looking to build financial security, life insurance can be both a protection tool and an income-generating asset. With life insurance, you can:

Protect Your Family: Life insurance ensures that your family is financially protected should the unexpected happen.

Build Savings Over Time: Policies with a cash value component, like whole and universal life insurance, can accumulate savings that grow over time, adding value to your policy.

Generate Income Opportunities: Cash value can be used as collateral, invested, or even withdrawn in certain situations, providing a potential income stream. Some policies also pay dividends, offering additional income.

HOW LIFE INSURANCE POLICIES WORK

When you purchase a life insurance policy, you'll select the coverage amount (the death benefit) and the type of policy that best suits your needs. Your premiums are based on factors like your age, health, and policy type. As long as you pay your premiums, the policy remains active, ensuring your beneficiaries will receive the death benefit.

Some life insurance policies, especially those with cash value, allow you to access a portion of the cash value through loans or withdrawals, which can be used for emergencies or investments. This feature opens up unique opportunities for those who want to build income while also enjoying the peace of mind that life insurance provides.

MOVING FORWARD

In this book, you'll discover how different types of life insurance policies work, learn how to maximize their potential for income generation, and explore the pros and cons of each method.

In the next chapter, we'll dive deeper into the various types of life insurance policies, breaking down each one to help you find the best fit for your financial goals.

2: DIFFERENT TYPES OF LIFE INSURANCE POLICIES

FINDING THE RIGHT POLICY FOR YOUR FINANCIAL GOALS

L ife insurance isn't a one-size-fits-all product. There are several types of life insurance policies, each with its own set of features, costs, and benefits. Choosing the right policy depends on your personal financial goals, the level of coverage you want for your family, and whether you're interested in using life insurance as a tool for building wealth.

In this chapter, we'll explore the primary types of life insurance policies—*Term Life Insurance, Whole Life Insurance,* and *Universal Life Insurance*—and discuss the unique features that each offers.

1. TERM LIFE INSURANCE: COVERAGE FOR A SET PERIOD

Term life insurance provides coverage for a specific period, typically ranging from 10 to 30 years. If you pass away during the term, your beneficiaries receive the death benefit. However, if you outlive the term, the policy expires, and no benefit is paid out.

Key Features:

Affordability: Term life is often the least expensive option, making it accessible for those on a budget.

Fixed Term: The coverage lasts only for the term you choose, after which the policy expires.

No Cash Value: Unlike other types, term life insurance doesn't accumulate cash value.

Best For: Individuals who need affordable coverage for a limited period, such as young families wanting financial protection until their children are grown.

2. WHOLE LIFE INSURANCE: LIFETIME COVERAGE WITH A CASH VALUE COMPONENT

Whole life insurance provides lifetime coverage, as long as you keep paying your premiums. One of its unique features is a cash value component that grows over time, often with a fixed interest rate. This cash value acts as a savings element, allowing you to borrow against it or even withdraw funds under certain conditions.

Key Features:

Lifetime Protection: Coverage remains active for life, guaranteeing a payout.

Cash Value Accumulation: A portion of your premiums goes into a cash value account, which grows tax-deferred.

Premium Stability: Premiums are usually fixed, offering long-term predictability.

Best For: Those looking for lifelong coverage with the option to build savings over time, making it a potential tool for estate planning and wealth transfer.

3. UNIVERSAL LIFE INSURANCE: FLEXIBILITY IN PREMIUMS AND CASH VALUE GROWTH

Universal life insurance offers lifetime coverage and a cash value component similar to whole life, but with added flexibility. You can adjust your premiums and death benefit (within certain limits) to suit your changing financial situation. This flexibility can make it appealing to those who want more control over their policy.

Key Features:

Adjustable Premiums: You can pay higher premiums to increase the cash value or reduce payments if needed.

Cash Value Growth: The cash value can grow based on either a fixed interest rate or an index-linked return.

Potential for Higher Returns: Some universal life policies allow cash value to grow faster based on market-linked options.

Best For: Those seeking flexibility in payments and death benefits, along with an interest in using the cash value component as an investment vehicle.

Comparing Policy Types: Key Considerations

Policy Type	Coverage Duration	Cash Value Growth	Premium Flexibility	Potential for Income Generation
Term Life	Fixed term (e.g., 10-30 years)	None	None	Minimal (coverage only)
Whole Life	Lifetime	Guaranteed, often fixed	Fixed premiums	Moderate (through cash value & dividends)
Universal Life	Lifetime	Variable or indexed (market-linked)	Adjustable	High (flexible cash value & loan potential)

4. OTHER TYPES: INDEXED AND VARIABLE LIFE INSURANCE

Beyond the main types, there are other life insurance products, like *Indexed Universal Life (IUL)* and *Variable Life Insurance:*

Indexed Universal Life (IUL): This is a form of universal life insurance where the cash value growth is linked to a stock market index, offering potential higher returns.

Variable Life Insurance: Offers investment options for the cash value component, where funds can be allocated into separate accounts similar to mutual funds, giving the policyholder direct exposure to the market.

Best For: Individuals with a higher risk tolerance who are looking to maximize cash value growth through investment options.

CHOOSING THE RIGHT POLICY

Selecting the right type of life insurance depends on your needs, budget, and long-term goals. If your primary goal is affordable, temporary protection, term life insurance might be the best choice. For those interested in building cash value and gaining access to the policy's savings, whole or universal life insurance may be more suitable.

Understanding these types and what each offers will help you make informed decisions about how life insurance can support your financial objectives. In the next chapter, we'll look at how life insurance policies can also serve as tools for income generation—an added benefit for those interested in using life insurance for wealth-building.

3: GENERATING INCOME WITH LIFE INSURANCE

TURNING YOUR POLICY INTO A WEALTH-BUILDING ASSET

While many people think of life insurance solely as a protective measure for their loved ones, certain types of life insurance policies can also serve as effective wealth-building tools. Through strategic management of your policy's cash value, dividends, and loan options, you can leverage life insurance to create additional income streams, fund investments, or supplement your retirement.

In this chapter, we'll explore the income-generating features that some life insurance policies offer, helping you understand how to transform your policy into a valuable financial asset.

1. CASH VALUE ACCUMULATION

Certain life insurance policies, such as whole life and universal life, include a *cash value component* that grows over time. This cash value functions similarly to a savings account, with part of your premium contributing to its growth. Because it grows on a tax-deferred basis, you won't have to pay taxes on the growth until you make withdrawals, making it an effective savings vehicle.

How It Generates Income:

Accessing Cash Value: You can withdraw from your cash value or take loans against it. These funds can be used to cover expenses, fund investments, or even supplement retirement income.

Tax Advantages: The tax-deferred nature of cash value growth allows it to accumulate more efficiently, letting you potentially draw on it as a tax-free income source in retirement.

2. POLICY LOANS: BORROWING AGAINST YOUR POLICY

One of the unique features of whole and universal life insurance policies is the ability to borrow against the cash value. Unlike traditional bank loans, policy loans don't require a credit check, and the loan interest rates are often lower. Moreover, since you're borrowing against your own policy, there's no strict repayment schedule, offering flexibility in how and when you repay.

How It Generates Income:

Funding Investments: Policy loans can be used as seed money for investment opportunities or to fund new ventures. For example, you could borrow against your cash value to invest in real estate or other income-generating assets.

Avoiding Traditional Loan Costs: By using policy loans, you can avoid higher interest rates or strict requirements of conventional loans, which can ultimately save money and increase cash flow.

3. EARNING DIVIDENDS ON PARTICIPATING POLICIES

Certain whole life policies, known as participating policies, may pay annual dividends to policyholders. These dividends are essentially a share of the insurance company's profits, distributed to eligible policyholders. While dividends are never guaranteed, they can provide a consistent source of income if you choose a policy from a reputable, financially strong insurer.

How It Generates Income:

Receiving Cash Payouts: You can take your dividends as cash payouts, providing you with an additional income stream without reducing your policy's death benefit or cash value.

Reinvesting for Compounded Growth: Alternatively, reinvesting dividends into your cash value can compound growth, allowing you to build your wealth over time. Later, this compounding effect could mean higher dividends or more cash value to borrow against or withdraw from.

4. LIFE SETTLEMENTS: SELLING YOUR POLICY FOR CASH

A *life settlement* is the sale of an active life insurance policy to a third party for a cash sum. While this option is generally considered by older policyholders who no longer need the death benefit, it can be a way to generate a significant cash payout, often greater than the cash value.

How It Generates Income:

Immediate Cash Payout: By selling your policy, you receive a lump sum payment that can be used for any purpose, from covering medical expenses to reinvesting in other assets.

Potential for Higher Returns: Life settlements can sometimes yield more money than the policy's cash surrender value, making it a profitable option for those who qualify and no longer require the death benefit.

5. SUPPLEMENTAL RETIREMENT INCOME

One of the most appealing benefits of cash value life insurance is its potential to supplement retirement income. You can structure your withdrawals or policy loans to receive steady payouts, turning your life insurance policy into an additional income stream that supports your lifestyle in retirement.

How It Generates Income:

Tax-Free Withdrawals: In many cases, cash value withdrawals can be taken out on a tax-free basis, giving you a steady source of tax-advantaged income during retirement.

Flexible Payouts: Unlike traditional retirement accounts, life insurance policies don't have required minimum distributions (RMDs), meaning you can withdraw funds according to your own needs and timelines.

CHOOSING THE RIGHT STRATEGY FOR INCOME GENERATION

The specific ways in which you can use life insurance for income generation depend on the type of policy you own and your financial goals. Cash value policies offer more flexibility and income potential than term policies, making them ideal for those interested in using life insurance as a financial asset. Understanding each option's benefits and potential downsides is key to maximizing your policy's earning potential.

In the next section, we'll uncover the mechanics of cash value accumulation and show you how to leverage this unique feature for long-term financial growth.

PART 2: UNDERSTANDING CASH VALUE AND INCOME POTENTIAL

4: CASH VALUE ACCUMULATION AND HOW IT WORKS

BUILDING WEALTH WITHIN YOUR LIFE INSURANCE POLICY

C ash value accumulation is a unique feature of certain permanent life insurance policies, such as whole life and universal life insurance. This feature allows a portion of your premium payments to grow over time, creating a cash reserve within your policy. Think of it as a built-in savings component that grows tax-deferred, helping you build wealth while providing life insurance coverage.

Understanding how cash value accumulation works is essential if you're aiming to leverage life insurance as an income-generating tool. In this chapter, we'll explain the basics of cash value, how it grows, and how it can become a valuable financial asset.

WHAT IS CASH VALUE?

Cash value is the investment or savings component of certain life insurance policies. Unlike term life insurance, which provides coverage for a set period with no savings feature, whole life and universal life policies include cash value that grows over time. A portion of each premium you pay is allocated to this cash value account, while the remainder covers the cost of insurance and other policy fees.

HOW CASH VALUE ACCUMULATES OVER TIME

The growth of cash value is fueled by a combination of your premium payments and compounding interest. Here's a breakdown of the core elements that contribute to cash value growth:

Premium Payments: A portion of each premium is allocated to the cash value after covering insurance costs and fees. The more you pay in premiums, the faster your cash value grows.

Interest and Dividends: For policies like whole life, the cash value earns interest at a fixed rate and may receive dividends. In a universal life policy, interest rates are adjustable based on prevailing market rates.

Investment Returns (VUL): In variable universal life policies, cash value is linked to investments. While this can lead to higher growth during market upswings, there is also risk of value decline if the market dips.

Cash value growth varies depending on the type of life insurance policy you choose:

Whole Life Insurance: Cash value grows at a fixed rate, providing a stable and predictable rate of return. Your policy's cash value grows through interest that's set by the insurer, making it a safe and conservative way to accumulate wealth.

Universal Life Insurance: Cash value growth is often tied to an index or market performance (in the case of indexed or variable universal life policies). This setup offers potential for higher returns, but the growth rate may fluctuate based on market conditions.

Cash value growth is tax-deferred, meaning you won't owe taxes on any growth until you withdraw or borrow against it. This tax advantage allows your cash value to accumulate more efficiently, similar to retirement accounts like a 401(k) or an IRA.

THE ROLE OF DIVIDENDS IN CASH VALUE ACCUMULATION (WHOLE LIFE)

For participating whole life policies, dividends can play a significant role in accelerating cash value growth. These dividends are typically a share of the insurer's profits, distributed to eligible policyholders. While dividends are not guaranteed, many established insurers pay them consistently.

How Dividends Can Be Used:

Reinvesting Dividends: You can reinvest dividends into the cash value, accelerating growth.

Taking Cash: Dividends can also be taken as cash payouts, providing an additional income stream.

Premium Reduction: Alternatively, dividends can be used to reduce premium payments, freeing up cash flow.

GROWTH OVER TIME: THE POWER OF COMPOUNDING

One of the most compelling aspects of cash value is its compounding effect. As the cash value grows, it generates interest on an increasingly larger amount, resulting in exponential growth over time.

Here's how compounding works in life insurance:

Early Growth Phase: In the initial years, cash value accumulation may feel slow as a larger portion of premiums covers policy expenses.

Accelerated Growth Phase: As the cash value grows, more of your premium and earned interest are added to the growing balance. Compounding takes effect, and the cash value begins to increase faster each year.

Long-Term Compounding: By keeping the policy in force over several decades, the compounding effect can result in a sizable cash value, offering both financial security and potential income.

The longer you keep your policy, the more pronounced this growth becomes. For this reason, policies with cash value work best as long-term financial assets, as compounding requires time to maximize its impact.

FACTORS INFLUENCING CASH VALUE GROWTH

The rate at which your cash value grows depends on a few important factors:

Premium Amount: Paying higher premiums increases the cash value faster. Whole life policies, in particular, benefit from regular and consistent premium payments.

Policy Type: Whole life policies grow at a fixed rate, while UL policies depend on market interest rates, and VUL policies fluctuate based on investments. Selecting the right policy type is crucial based on your cash growth goals and risk tolerance.

Dividends: Participating whole life policies may pay dividends, which can be reinvested to grow cash value or taken as income. Reinvesting dividends can lead to faster cash value accumulation.

Loan Activity: If you borrow against your policy, the outstanding loan balance will reduce the effective growth of cash value. Repaying loans as soon as possible helps maintain growth momentum.

CASH VALUE ACCUMULATION STRATEGIES

To maximize cash value growth, consider these strategies:

Choose Paid-Up Additions: Some whole life policies allow you to purchase additional coverage, or "paid-up additions," which increase both the death benefit and cash value. This can accelerate cash value accumulation.

Pay Extra Premiums: Many policies allow for additional premium payments, which go directly toward cash value and can boost growth.

Leave Dividends in the Policy: Reinvesting dividends compounds their effect on cash value over time, increasing both the death benefit and cash value.

Minimize Loans and Withdrawals: Avoid frequent withdrawals or loans, which reduce the compounding power of your cash value. Keeping loans to a minimum ensures maximum growth potential.

CALCULATING CASH VALUE GROWTH

To get a sense of how your cash value will grow, request projections from your insurer or use online calculators. These tools factor in premium payments, compounding interest, and potential dividends to project future values. Remember, projections are estimates; actual growth may vary based on policy terms and market conditions.

BENEFITS OF CASH VALUE ACCUMULATION FOR INCOME

Accumulating cash value has multiple benefits, making it a powerful financial asset:

Income Stream Potential: Cash value can be accessed for supplemental income in retirement or emergencies through withdrawals and loans.

Loan Collateral: You can borrow against your cash value at competitive rates, often lower than conventional loans, allowing you to leverage your policy for other investments.

BENEFITS OF CASH VALUE ACCUMULATION FOR INCOME GENERATION

Cash value accumulation can be a powerful financial tool for several reasons:

Tax Advantages: Cash value grows tax-deferred, making it a tax-efficient savings tool.

Financial Flexibility: The cash value provides a source of accessible funds, allowing you to cover emergency expenses, fund investments, or even supplement retirement income.

Potential for Passive Income: Dividends and cash withdrawals provide potential income streams, giving you financial freedom beyond the death benefit.

POTENTIAL DRAWBACKS AND CONSIDERATIONS

While cash value policies offer valuable benefits, there are also factors to consider:

Slow Initial Growth: In the early years, cash value growth may be minimal as most premiums go toward policy costs. It usually takes several years before the cash value grows significantly.

Fees and Costs: Permanent life insurance policies with cash value are typically more expensive than term policies. High fees can impact growth, particularly in the early stages.

Opportunity Costs: The money you put into a cash value policy might yield higher returns if invested elsewhere, depending on your financial goals and risk tolerance.

IS CASH VALUE RIGHT FOR YOU?

Cash value policies are most beneficial for those with long-term financial goals who want both life insurance protection and an asset that grows over time. If you're seeking a flexible financial tool that offers both security and income potential, a cash value policy may be an ideal fit.

In the next chapter, we'll explore the mechanics of accessing your cash value, the various options available, and how to strategically leverage these funds to meet your financial goals without compromising the long-term benefits of your policy.

5: ACCESSING YOUR CASH VALUE

WITHDRAWALS, LOANS, AND SURRENDER

L ife insurance can be more than just a safety net for your family; it can be a source of accessible funds through the cash value accumulated over time. Cash value life insurance policies allow you to access money for various purposes, offering flexibility in times of need, opportunities for investments, or even a way to fund your retirement.

In this chapter, we'll explore how cash value accumulates, when it becomes accessible, and the main ways you can leverage it: through policy loans, withdrawals, or even surrendering the policy. While these methods provide valuable options, each one has pros and cons that should be carefully considered to avoid impacting the future value of your policy.

HOW LONG DOES IT TAKE TO BUILD CASH VALUE IN LIFE INSURANCE?

Cash value doesn't build overnight. Generally, it can take several years—anywhere from two to five years—for the cash value to start accumulating in a meaningful way. The speed at which it grows depends largely on the type of life insurance policy you have:

Whole Life Insurance: Builds cash value at a steady, predictable rate based on a fixed interest rate. Although it may take longer to accumulate significant cash value, whole life insurance offers stability and consistency.

Universal Life Insurance: Provides more flexibility in cash value accumulation, as its growth is typically linked to market interest rates or a chosen index. However, returns can vary depending on market conditions.

Variable Universal Life Insurance: Has the highest growth potential, as its cash value can increase based on the performance of investment accounts. This option carries more risk, as cash value can decrease in a poor market, but it may offer faster accumulation when markets are strong.

ACCESSING YOUR CASH VALUE

Once cash value has built up, it becomes an asset you can use for various purposes. Here's a breakdown of the primary ways to access your cash value:

1. POLICY LOANS: BORROWING AGAINST YOUR CASH VALUE

One of the most popular ways to access cash value is through a policy loan, which allows you to borrow from the policy's cash value without triggering taxes. Because the loan is treated as an advance on your death benefit, it's considered tax-free. However, it's important to understand the terms and implications:

Interest Charges: Policy loans come with interest, typically lower than a traditional bank loan. Although payments are flexible, if you don't pay back the loan, interest continues to accumulate, reducing the policy's death benefit.

Impact on Death Benefit: If a loan remains unpaid at the time of your passing, the outstanding amount will be deducted from the death benefit, reducing the payout for your beneficiaries.

When It's Useful: Policy loans can be helpful for funding major purchases, investing in opportunities, or meeting unexpected expenses without the need to go through traditional credit checks.

2. WITHDRAWALS: DIRECT ACCESS TO CASH VALUE

Cash value withdrawals provide another way to access the funds in your policy, generally tax-free up to the amount you've paid in premiums. Withdrawals, however, reduce the available cash value and the death benefit proportionally.

Tax Implications: Withdrawals are typically tax-free up to the total of premiums you've paid. If you withdraw more than this amount, the excess becomes taxable as ordinary income.

Impact on Policy Value: Unlike loans, withdrawals permanently decrease both the cash value and the death benefit of your policy. For instance, if you withdraw $10,000, your beneficiaries' payout will be reduced by that amount.

When It's Useful: Withdrawals are a good option for one-time needs, such as paying for education expenses, making home improvements, or supplementing retirement income.

3. SURRENDERING THE POLICY: CASHING OUT ENTIRELY

Surrendering your life insurance policy is an option if you decide you no longer need the coverage or prefer to access the entire cash value. When you surrender, you're effectively canceling the policy and receiving a lump sum, known as the cash surrender value.

Surrender Fees: Many policies have fees for surrendering, particularly in the early years. It's crucial to review your policy to understand any potential charges.

Tax Considerations: Any amount you receive from surrendering your policy above the total premiums paid is considered taxable income.

Loss of Coverage: Surrendering means that your life insurance coverage ends, leaving your beneficiaries without a death benefit. This option should be considered only if you have other financial resources or no longer need the coverage.

When It's Useful: Surrendering might be suitable if you have no ongoing need for insurance, are facing significant financial hardship, or prefer to invest the cash value elsewhere.

WEIGHING THE PROS AND CONS OF ACCESSING CASH VALUE

Using your cash value provides you with financial flexibility, but each method impacts your policy's overall value differently. Here are a few key points to consider when deciding how to access cash value:

Loans vs. Withdrawals: Loans allow you to keep your policy active and death benefit largely intact, while withdrawals provide immediate funds but permanently reduce both the death benefit and cash value.

Tax Implications: Loans are generally tax-free, whereas withdrawals may be subject to taxes depending on the amount withdrawn.

Impact on Future Benefits: Any decrease in cash value—whether through loans, withdrawals, or surrendering—affects the overall growth of the policy and reduces the payout to beneficiaries.

MAKING THE MOST OF YOUR CASH VALUE

Accessing cash value can be a strategic tool if used wisely. Whether it's to take advantage of investment opportunities, cover large expenses, or supplement retirement, your policy's cash value can be an asset that works for you. But remember, these options should be aligned with your long-term financial goals and carefully weighed against the impact on your policy's future benefits.

In the next chapter, we'll explore the various ways to select a policy type with the best potential for income generation, so you can maximize the benefits of your life insurance as a wealth-building tool.

6: CHOOSING THE RIGHT TYPE FOR INCOME POTENTIAL

MAXIMIZING YOUR POLICY'S FINANCIAL BENEFITS

C hoosing the right type of life insurance policy can significantly impact your ability to generate income and grow wealth over time. With options ranging from whole life to universal life insurance, each type offers unique advantages and drawbacks. This chapter will guide you through key considerations to help you select a policy that aligns with your income goals and long-term financial needs.

UNDERSTANDING YOUR INCOME GOALS

Before selecting a policy, clarify your income objectives with life insurance. Are you looking for:

Steady Cash Flow: Do you want a consistent income stream through dividends or loan access?

Tax-Deferred Growth: Are you more focused on accumulating tax-deferred cash value?

Flexible Access to Funds: Is the option to withdraw or borrow against your policy important for your financial planning?

By defining your goals, you can choose a policy type that aligns with how you plan to use the accumulated value.

COMPARING POLICY TYPES FOR INCOME POTENTIAL

Each type of life insurance policy has unique attributes that can affect its potential for income generation. Here's an overview of the three primary options:

1. WHOLE LIFE INSURANCE:

Known for stability, whole life policies provide guaranteed cash value growth and a fixed death benefit. They're particularly appealing for those seeking a predictable, conservative option for income.

Dividends: Participating whole life policies often pay dividends, which can be taken as cash or reinvested. Although dividends aren't guaranteed, many insurers have a history of paying them consistently.

Best for: Those seeking a reliable cash accumulation vehicle and conservative income stream potential through dividends.

2. UNIVERSAL LIFE INSURANCE (UL):

UL policies offer more flexibility than whole life, with cash value growth based on interest rates or investment performance (in the case of variable or indexed UL). This flexibility provides potential for higher returns but with some exposure to market risks.

Adjustable Premiums: You can adjust your premium payments within limits, allowing for potential cash flow adjustments.

Best for: Those interested in potential higher cash value growth and who are comfortable with some market exposure.

3. VARIABLE UNIVERSAL LIFE INSURANCE (VUL):

With VUL, the cash value is invested in a selection of mutual fund-like sub-accounts, offering the highest growth potential among permanent policies. However, the value fluctuates with market performance, making it riskier.

Investment-Based Growth: The cash value can grow significantly if investments perform well, but it may decline during downturns.

Best for: Experienced investors who are comfortable with risk and seek greater returns over the long term.

PROS AND CONS OF EACH POLICY TYPE FOR INCOME

Policy Type	Pros	Cons
Whole Life	Steady cash value growth; Potential for dividends	Higher premiums; Slower initial growth
Universal Life	Flexible premiums; Cash value growth based on interest rates	Growth tied to market rates; Requires careful monitoring
Variable Universal Life	Potential for high returns; Variety of investment options	Market risk exposure; Cash value can fluctuate

Selecting the right policy depends on your risk tolerance, financial goals, and the degree of flexibility you need in accessing cash.

KEY CONSIDERATIONS FOR MAXIMIZING INCOME POTENTIAL

Several factors will influence the income potential of your life insurance policy:

Premium Affordability: Higher premiums contribute to quicker cash value growth, but they also require a long-term commitment. Make sure you can comfortably afford the premiums without compromising other financial priorities.

Tax Implications: Cash value withdrawals, loans, and dividends are generally tax-free up to the total premiums paid but can become taxable if they exceed that amount. Plan your withdrawals and policy loans accordingly.

Market Sensitivity: If you choose UL or VUL policies, be prepared for fluctuating cash value based on market conditions. For steady growth, whole life policies may be more suitable.

Time Horizon: Cash value grows best over a long period, making these policies ideal for those with longer investment horizons. The compounding effect on cash value builds significantly over time, so patience is essential.

USING RIDERS TO ENHANCE INCOME POTENTIAL

Riders are policy add-ons that can increase the flexibility and income potential of a life insurance policy. Consider adding the following riders for enhanced benefits:

Accelerated Death Benefit Rider: Provides early access to a portion of the death benefit if diagnosed with a terminal illness.

Paid-Up Additions Rider: Allows you to buy additional coverage that grows cash value faster, enhancing dividends and cash flow potential.

Waiver of Premium Rider: Waives premiums in case of disability, ensuring your cash value continues to grow without additional out-of-pocket costs.

These riders can make your policy more adaptable to changing financial needs while also increasing the income potential over time.

PRACTICAL TIPS FOR POLICY SELECTION

Consult with an Expert: Work with a financial advisor specializing in life insurance to match a policy to your specific income and growth goals.

Compare Policies: Request detailed quotes and projections for each type of policy to evaluate cash value accumulation rates and long-term income potential.

Review Financial Stability of Insurers: Choose an insurer with a strong financial rating to ensure the reliability of dividend payments and cash value growth.

CHOOSING THE BEST PATH FOR INCOME WITH LIFE INSUR-

ANCE

Life insurance can be more than just a safety net for your loved ones; it can be a strategic tool for building wealth and generating income. By choosing the right policy type and understanding its income potential, you can position yourself to leverage life insurance as a valuable part of your financial portfolio.

In the next chapter, we'll explore how you can use this cash value as collateral for policy loans, allowing you to borrow against it strategically.

7: TAKING A LOAN FROM YOUR POLICY

USING CASH VALUE AS COLLATERAL FOR POLICY LOANS

One of the valuable benefits of certain life insurance policies is the ability to borrow against your cash value. This feature provides flexibility and liquidity, allowing you to access cash for investment while keeping your policy intact. In this chapter, we'll look at how policy loans work, how they can be a strategic financial tool, and what to consider before borrowing against your cash value.

HOW POLICY LOANS WORK

When you have a life insurance policy with cash value, like whole life or universal life, you can typically borrow up to a certain percentage of the accumulated cash value. This loan uses the cash value as collateral, meaning your policy's value and benefits remain intact while you access funds. Here's how the process generally works:

Loan Application: Contact your insurer to check your available cash value and request a policy loan. The application process is usually simple, with minimal paperwork.

Loan Amount: Most insurers allow you to borrow between 70%

and 90% of the cash value, depending on the policy terms.

Repayment Flexibility: Policy loans often come with flexible repayment terms, allowing you to pay at your own pace or even defer payments indefinitely. However, interest will accumulate on the loan balance.

Interest Rates: Policy loans typically have competitive interest rates, often lower than traditional bank loans. Rates can be fixed or variable, depending on the policy type and insurer.

BENEFITS OF BORROWING AGAINST CASH VALUE

Using cash value as collateral offers unique advantages, making it a popular choice for those seeking flexible funding:

No Credit Check: Because the loan is secured by your own cash value, insurers don't require a credit check, making this option accessible even for those with low credit scores.

Speed and Ease: Policy loans are generally faster and easier to obtain than conventional loans, with quick approval and access to funds.

Tax-Free Funds: Loans from life insurance policies are not typically considered taxable income, allowing you to access cash without facing tax consequences.

No Impact on Death Benefit (If Repaid): If you repay the loan with interest, the full death benefit remains intact for your beneficiaries.

POTENTIAL USES FOR POLICY LOANS

Policy loans can be a versatile financial resource for various situations. Here are some common uses:

Emergency Expenses: For unforeseen costs, like medical bills or urgent home repairs, a policy loan offers quick access to funds without disrupting your policy.

Debt Consolidation: Policy loans often have lower interest rates than credit cards or personal loans, making them a practical option for consolidating high-interest debt.

Investment Opportunities: Some use policy loans to invest in new ventures, real estate, or education. The returns from these investments can sometimes exceed the loan's interest rate, making it a strategic choice.

Supplemental Income: Policy loans can also be used as a source of retirement income, providing cash flow while keeping your investments intact.

REPAYING POLICY LOANS

While policy loans offer flexible repayment terms, it's important to have a plan for repayment. Here's why:

Interest Accumulation: Policy loans accrue interest, which compounds if left unpaid. The longer the loan remains unpaid, the more interest you'll owe, potentially reducing the value of your policy.

Death Benefit Reduction: If the loan is not repaid before the policyholder's death, the outstanding balance will be deducted from the death benefit, leaving less for beneficiaries.

Risk of Policy Lapse: If the loan balance plus interest exceeds the cash value, the policy could lapse, resulting in a loss of coverage and potential tax consequences. Regular repayment helps prevent this risk.

CONSIDERATIONS BEFORE TAKING A POLICY LOAN

While policy loans are a useful tool, it's essential to weigh the pros and cons to make an informed decision. Key factors to consider include:

Impact on Future Growth: Borrowing against your cash value may slow the overall growth of the cash value due to reduced compounding.

Loan Interest Rate: Evaluate whether the interest rate on the policy loan is favorable compared to other financing options.

Long-Term Plans: If your policy is a significant part of your estate or retirement plan, ensure that taking a loan aligns with these goals.

Loan Alternatives: Explore other options, like personal loans or lines of credit, to determine if a policy loan is the most strategic choice for your situation.

HOW TO MAXIMIZE BENEFITS AND MINIMIZE RISKS

By approaching policy loans strategically, you can maximize their benefits and minimize any potential downsides. Here are some strategies to keep in mind:

Borrow Only What You Need: Avoid over-borrowing by taking only the necessary amount to meet your financial needs. This keeps the loan balance manageable and reduces interest costs.

Plan for Repayment: Even though repayment is flexible, establishing a regular repayment schedule can help control interest costs and keep your policy in good standing.

Monitor Your Policy's Health: Keep track of the policy's cash value, loan balance, and interest charges to ensure it doesn't approach lapse status. Regularly reviewing your policy with an advisor can help manage this risk.

Consider Partial Repayments: If you're unable to repay the full amount, making partial payments can help keep interest under control and protect the policy's value.

POLICY LOANS VS. WITHDRAWALS: CHOOSING THE RIGHT OPTION

If you're considering accessing your cash value, you might wonder whether to take a loan or a direct withdrawal. Here's a quick comparison to help you decide:

Policy Loan: Allows you to access cash without reducing the cash value permanently, and the loan is not taxable. However, unpaid loans can reduce the death benefit and accrue interest.

Withdrawal: Directly reduces the cash value and may impact the policy's future growth, but it doesn't require repayment. Withdrawals can also have tax implications depending on the policy and withdrawal amount.

Generally, policy loans are preferable when you plan to repay, while withdrawals may be a better choice if you don't intend to repay the funds. Consulting with a financial advisor can clarify which option best aligns with your goals.

PLANNING AHEAD FOR A POLICY LOAN

If you anticipate needing access to funds in the future, there are steps you can take now to make policy loans more effective:

Choose a Policy with High Cash Value Potential: Certain policies, like whole life or variable universal life, tend to build cash value faster, providing a larger loan base.

Pay Premiums Regularly: Consistent premium payments help maximize cash value accumulation, giving you greater access to funds.

Add a Paid-Up Additions Rider: If available, a paid-up additions rider can accelerate cash value growth, expanding your borrowing power over time.

Using your cash value as collateral for policy loans provides a unique way to meet financial needs while maintaining the core benefits of your life insurance. With careful planning, policy loans can serve as a flexible, tax-efficient financing option that protects both your policy and your financial goals.

Next, we'll explore the benefits and risks of borrowing against your policy, diving into real-world scenarios to better understand when—and when not—to take a policy loan.

8: BENEFITS AND RISKS OF POLICY LOANS

WEIGHING THE PROS AND CONS OF POLICY LOANS

Borrowing against a life insurance policy is an attractive option for many people, offering flexibility, tax advantages, and easy access to cash without strict repayment terms. However, policy loans also come with unique considerations that are crucial to understand to make informed choices.

In this chapter, we'll explore the key benefits and risks of policy loans, helping you decide if and when this approach fits your financial goals.

KEY BENEFITS OF POLICY LOANS

Borrowing from your life insurance policy can provide several strategic benefits, especially when compared to other loan types:

Immediate Access to Funds: Policy loans don't involve lengthy approval processes or credit checks, meaning you can access cash quickly for unexpected expenses, debt consolidation, or even investment opportunities.

Tax-Free Cash Access: Unlike some other forms of borrowing, policy loans aren't considered taxable income as long as the policy remains active. This provides a tax-efficient way to access funds without increasing your annual tax burden.

Competitive Interest Rates: Most policy loans come with relatively low, fixed interest rates, especially compared to credit cards or personal loans. These rates can make policy loans a cost-effective option for funding financial needs.

Flexible Repayment Options: Unlike traditional loans, policy loans don't come with rigid repayment schedules. You can choose to repay at your own pace, and in some cases, repayment can even be deferred, although interest will still accrue.

No Impact on Credit Score: Since policy loans aren't reported to credit bureaus, they won't affect your credit score. This makes them ideal for people who may need cash but want to avoid credit-related scrutiny.

KEY RISKS OF BORROWING AGAINST YOUR POLICY

While policy loans offer distinct advantages, they also come with potential risks. It's essential to understand these risks before deciding to borrow:

Interest Accumulation: Policy loans accrue interest, which compounds if left unpaid. Over time, this can reduce your policy's cash value and increase the total amount you owe, potentially offsetting the benefits of borrowing in the first place.

Reduced Death Benefit: Any unpaid loan balance, including accrued interest, will be deducted from your policy's death benefit. This means that if the loan isn't repaid by the time you pass away, your beneficiaries will receive a reduced payout.

Risk of Policy Lapse: If your loan balance plus interest exceeds your policy's cash value, your policy could lapse. When a policy lapses, coverage ends, and you risk losing both the death benefit and any accumulated cash value. You may also face tax consequences in some cases if the policy lapses with an outstanding loan balance.

Missed Growth Opportunities: When you take a loan against your cash value, you effectively reduce the amount available to compound and grow. This could lead to lower overall returns on your policy, especially in high-growth scenarios where cash value growth is significant.

EVALUATING YOUR PERSONAL SITUATION

Whether a policy loan is right for you depends on your financial goals and situation. Here are some scenarios to consider:

Short-Term Cash Needs: For short-term financial needs, a policy loan can be an ideal solution. If you have a plan to repay the loan within a reasonable timeframe, you'll minimize interest costs and protect your policy's value.

Funding Large Purchases or Investments: Some individuals use policy loans to fund significant investments, like real estate or education. This strategy can work well if the investment's return exceeds the loan interest rate. However, it's essential to be cautious and evaluate potential returns realistically.

Avoiding Credit-Based Loans: If you prefer not to use credit-based loans due to high interest rates or credit score concerns, a policy loan can offer an accessible and secure option.

PLANNING REPAYMENT STRATEGICALLY

While policy loans come with flexible repayment terms, having a plan for repayment can help protect your policy's value. Here are some tips for managing repayment:

Consider Regular Payments: Making regular payments toward the loan balance, even if small, helps keep the loan from compounding excessively and protects the cash value.

Use Dividends to Offset Interest: If you have a participating policy that earns dividends, you may be able to use these to cover interest payments. This can help maintain the loan balance and prevent cash value depletion.

Avoid Prolonged Non-Payment: Although you're not required to make regular payments, a long-term unpaid balance can diminish your policy's benefits. Try to make payments as your budget allows to keep the loan under control.

WHEN TO AVOID A POLICY LOAN

There are certain situations when it may be better to avoid taking a policy loan altogether. These include:

If You Don't Have a Repayment Plan: Borrowing without a realistic repayment plan could lead to long-term financial strain, reduced benefits, and possible policy lapse.

If You Depend Heavily on the Death Benefit: If your beneficiaries rely on the full death benefit amount, a loan that risks reducing the payout could impact their future financial stability.

If You Have Other Low-Cost Loan Options: If you qualify for low-interest personal loans or credit lines, consider those options before borrowing against your life insurance. This can help preserve your policy's cash value for future needs or retirement.

UNDERSTANDING THE COST OF COMPOUND INTEREST

It's important to understand how interest accrues on policy loans. Unlike simple interest, compound interest can grow quickly, especially if left unpaid over a long period. Here's an example of how compound interest works:

Example: Let's say you borrow $10,000 from your policy at an interest rate of 5%. If you don't make payments, the interest will continue to compound annually, increasing the loan balance. After five years, the unpaid balance would grow to approximately $12,763 due to compounding.

This example highlights the importance of planning for loan repayment to keep interest from eroding your policy's value.

MAKING AN INFORMED DECISION

Taking a policy loan can be a powerful tool if used wisely, but it's important to weigh both the benefits and risks. Here are a few questions to ask yourself:

· Are you borrowing to grow your wealth?
· Can I realistically repay the loan, and how soon?
· Will the reduced cash value or death benefit impact my financial or family goals?
· Are there alternative ways to fund this need that may be more cost-effective?

Taking the time to consider these questions will help you make a well-informed choice and maximize the value of your life insurance policy as a financial asset.

Understanding the benefits and risks of policy loans allows you to make strategic decisions that protect both your policy's value and your long-term financial stability. In the next section, we'll explore dividends and earnings, delving into how participating policies generate additional income that can further enhance your financial flexibility and returns.

PART 3: DIVIDENDS AND EARNINGS

9: UNDERSTANDING DIVIDENDS AND HOW THEY WORK

LEVERAGING DIVIDENDS TO BOOST YOUR LIFE INSURANCE BENEFITS

D ividends can be an enticing feature of certain life insurance policies, offering policyholders an opportunity to earn extra income or reinvest in their policy. But understanding how dividends work—and how they can benefit you—is essential to maximize your policy's potential. In this chapter, we'll explore what dividends are, how they're paid out, and ways to use them to your advantage.

WHAT ARE DIVIDENDS?

Dividends are essentially a share of the profits paid to policyholders by insurance companies, typically mutual insurers. These companies distribute dividends as a way of sharing excess profits with their policyholders, particularly those who own *participating* whole life insurance policies. Not all policies pay dividends, so it's crucial to know if your policy is designed to participate in these potential earnings.

HOW DO DIVIDENDS WORK?

Dividends come from the surplus generated by an insurance company. This surplus occurs when a company earns more than it needs to cover claims, expenses, and future liabilities. The company will often allocate a portion of this surplus to policyholders in the form of dividends, calculated based on several factors:

Investment Performance: Insurance companies invest premiums in various assets like bonds, stocks, and real estate. Good investment returns contribute to higher dividends.

Claims Experience: If fewer policyholders make claims than expected, the company's expenses are lower, resulting in more funds available for dividends.

Operational Efficiency: Efficient management and lower operating costs also contribute to an insurer's profitability, which may increase dividends.

Dividends are usually declared once a year and can fluctuate based on the company's financial performance. Importantly, dividends are not guaranteed and depend on the insurer's profitability and policy terms.

TYPES OF POLICIES THAT PAY DIVIDENDS

Not all life insurance policies are dividend-eligible. Dividends are typically associated with *participating* whole life policies issued by mutual insurance companies. Here are the primary types of policies that may pay dividends:

Participating Whole Life Insurance: This is the most common type of life insurance policy that pays dividends. Policyholders essentially have partial ownership in the insurer, entitling them to a portion of the profits.

Some Universal Life Policies: Although less common, certain universal life policies may offer dividends. It's essential to review the policy terms or speak to an insurance advisor to confirm if your universal life policy is dividend-eligible.

Knowing whether your policy pays dividends can help you make informed choices about how to use these additional funds.

OPTIONS FOR USING DIVIDENDS

When dividends are paid, you usually have several options for how to use them. Let's look at the most common ways policyholders manage their dividends:

Cash Payout: You can take dividends as cash, which can be used as supplemental income. This is ideal if you want immediate access to the funds and don't wish to reinvest in your policy.

Premium Reduction: Dividends can be used to reduce or cover premium payments. This option helps lower your out-of-pocket expenses and can be a convenient way to manage cash flow without affecting your policy's cash value.

Purchase Paid-Up Additions: Dividends can be reinvested to purchase additional coverage, known as paid-up additions. These additions increase both the cash value and the death benefit, enhancing your policy's long-term growth potential.

Accumulate at Interest: Some insurers offer an option to let dividends accumulate at interest. Here, the dividends remain with the insurer and earn a specified interest rate, allowing them to grow over time. This option is suitable if you want a low-risk way to build savings.

Loan Repayment: Dividends can also be directed toward repaying any outstanding policy loans. This option helps you manage debt without additional out-of-pocket expenses and can be beneficial if you're looking to reduce loan balances gradually.

REINVESTING DIVIDENDS FOR MAXIMUM GROWTH

For those focused on long-term financial growth, reinvesting dividends—such as through paid-up additions—can be a powerful strategy. Reinvested dividends can accelerate the accumulation of cash value, increase the death benefit, and offer a compounding effect over time. By reinvesting dividends, you essentially put your earnings back to work, creating a snowball effect that boosts the overall policy value.

Example: If you receive $500 in annual dividends and reinvest them to buy paid-up additions, those additions contribute to your cash value and increase the overall policy death benefit. Each year, your dividends compound as they are based on a larger policy value, creating a continuous growth cycle.

TAX CONSIDERATIONS FOR DIVIDENDS

In most cases, dividends from life insurance policies are considered a return of premium and aren't subject to income tax as long as they don't exceed the total premiums paid into the policy.

However, if dividends are left to accumulate at interest or taken as cash after surpassing premium amounts, they may become taxable. It's a good idea to consult a tax advisor to understand the implications of taking dividends in different forms.

POTENTIAL DRAWBACKS OF DIVIDENDS

While dividends can be an advantage, there are also some factors to be mindful of:

Dividend Variability: Dividends aren't guaranteed, and the amount can fluctuate yearly. If you rely heavily on dividends to cover premiums or as an income source, this variability could affect your financial plans.

Reinvestment Costs: While purchasing paid-up additions can be beneficial for policy growth, it may come with additional costs or fees. Reviewing these fees can help you evaluate whether reinvesting is worthwhile.

Inflation Impact: Dividend values might not always keep pace with inflation, especially if the insurer's investment returns or surplus declines. If you're relying on dividends as a cash source, this can affect your purchasing power over time.

IS A DIVIDEND-PAYING POLICY RIGHT FOR YOU?

If you're considering a dividend-paying life insurance policy, here are some questions to guide your decision:

Do you prefer flexible income options?: Dividend-paying policies offer multiple ways to use funds, making them ideal for those who value flexibility.

Are you focused on building cash value?: Reinvesting dividends helps maximize cash value growth, making a dividend-paying policy suitable if you're looking for long-term wealth accumulation.

How do you view policy stability?: While dividends aren't guaranteed, mutual insurance companies tend to have a long track record of paying dividends. If you're comfortable with potential fluctuations, these policies can be a valuable addition to a financial plan.

Do you understand the tax implications?: Knowing the tax treatment of dividends, especially if taken as cash or left to accumulate at interest, is essential to avoid unexpected tax liabilities.

MAKING THE MOST OF DIVIDENDS

Understanding how dividends work—and leveraging them to your benefit—can make a significant difference in your life insurance strategy. Whether you choose to take dividends as cash, reinvest them, or use them to reduce premiums, dividends can provide a steady and valuable financial benefit.

In the next chapter, we'll take a closer look at how to turn dividends into actual income, exploring strategies to use your policy's earnings as part of a broader financial plan.

10: HOW TO RECEIVE DIVIDENDS AS INCOME

STRATEGIES FOR TAPPING INTO YOUR LIFE INSURANCE DIVIDENDS

Dividends from your life insurance policy can provide a valuable source of income, enhancing your financial flexibility and stability. In this chapter, we'll explore how to access these dividends effectively, whether you want to take them as cash or use them to bolster your policy's value.

Understanding the options available will empower you to make informed decisions about how to use your dividends to support your financial goals.

CASH PAYMENTS: THE MOST DIRECT METHOD

One of the simplest ways to receive dividends is by opting for cash payments. When you choose this method, the insurance company pays out your dividends directly to you, providing immediate access to those funds. This option can be especially appealing if you need extra income for monthly expenses, emergencies, or discretionary spending.

Steps to Receive Cash Dividends:

Notify Your Insurer: Inform your insurance provider that you want to receive your dividends in cash. This is typically done at the time you purchase the policy or during the annual dividend declaration.

Confirm Payment Frequency: Dividends are usually paid annually, but some insurers may offer semi-annual or quarterly payments. Choose a frequency that aligns with your financial needs.

Keep Track of Tax Implications: While dividends are often not subject to income tax up to the total amount of premiums paid, any excess amount or accumulated interest may be taxable. Consult a tax advisor for clarification.

USING DIVIDENDS TO OFFSET PREMIUM PAYMENTS

Instead of taking cash, you can use your dividends to reduce or eliminate your premium payments. This option can ease your financial burden and free up cash for other expenses or investments.

How to Utilize Dividends for Premium Reduction:

Select the Option During Policy Setup: When purchasing your policy, indicate that you want dividends applied to premiums. This choice ensures dividends automatically offset your future premium obligations.

Monitor Your Policy Balance: Regularly review your policy statements to understand how much of your dividend is applied to premiums, ensuring you stay informed about your policy's status.

Using dividends to pay premiums is a strategic move for those looking to maintain coverage while managing their budget effectively.

REINVESTING DIVIDENDS FOR FUTURE GROWTH

If your primary goal is long-term wealth accumulation, reinvesting your dividends to purchase paid-up additions can significantly enhance your policy's cash value and death benefit. This approach not only strengthens your policy but also provides more significant returns over time.

Steps to Reinvest Dividends:

Choose Paid-Up Additions: Instruct your insurance company to reinvest dividends into paid-up additions. These additions create additional cash value and increase your death benefit without requiring further premium payments.

Watch the Compounding Effect: By reinvesting dividends, you allow the additional cash value to grow, generating future dividends and enhancing your overall policy value.

This strategy is particularly effective for those focused on long-term financial growth, as it leverages the power of compounding.

ACCUMULATING DIVIDENDS WITH INTEREST

Some insurers allow policyholders to accumulate dividends at interest, which can be an attractive option if you prefer to defer receiving cash while still earning growth on those funds.

Understanding the Accumulation Option:

Opt for Accumulation: When setting up your policy, choose the option to have dividends accumulate with interest rather than take them as cash.

Interest Rates and Growth: The insurer will apply a specified interest rate to the accumulated dividends, allowing your earnings to grow over time.

Accessing Accumulated Dividends: You can typically access accumulated dividends at any time by requesting a withdrawal or applying them toward premiums.

Accumulating dividends with interest is suitable for those who don't need immediate cash and prefer to allow their funds to grow for future needs.

EVALUATING YOUR DIVIDEND INCOME STRATEGY

To determine the best way to receive dividends as income, consider your financial situation and long-term goals. Ask yourself the following questions:

Do you need immediate cash flow?: If you require regular income to meet expenses, cash payments might be your best option.

Are you focused on reducing out-of-pocket costs?: Using dividends to offset premiums can alleviate financial pressure while keeping your policy in force.

Do you want to maximize growth potential?: If your goal is to enhance your policy's value over time, consider reinvesting dividends for paid-up additions or accumulating them with interest.

By aligning your dividend income strategy with your financial objectives, you can make the most of this valuable benefit.

MAKING DIVIDENDS WORK FOR YOU

Dividends from your life insurance policy can be a powerful tool for income generation and financial stability. By understanding the various ways to access and utilize these dividends, you can make strategic choices that align with your overall financial plan.

Whether you choose cash payments, premium reductions, reinvestment, or accumulation, being proactive in managing your dividends can enhance your financial well-being.

In the next chapter, we'll dive into both approaches—reinvesting for compounding growth or taking payouts for instant access to funds—so you can decide which option aligns best with your financial goals and wealth-building objectives.

11: REINVESTING DIVIDENDS VS. TAKING PAYOUTS

MAKING THE MOST OF YOUR LIFE INSURANCE FOR WEALTH BUILDING

For individuals looking to maximize the earning potential of their life insurance policy, understanding how to manage dividends effectively is crucial. When your life insurance policy generates dividends, you have two main choices: reinvest them for compounded growth or take them as cash payouts to meet immediate financial needs. Each approach has unique advantages, and choosing the right one can significantly impact your wealth-building journey.

In this chapter, we'll explore these options in detail, helping you decide the best path to grow your wealth and reach your financial goals.

THE CASE FOR REINVESTING DIVIDENDS

Reinvesting dividends within your life insurance policy can be a powerful way to grow your wealth over time. By choosing this option, you allow your policy's cash value and death benefit to increase steadily, potentially creating a robust foundation for future financial opportunities.

Increased Cash Value: Reinvesting dividends often means using them to purchase "paid-up additions." These additions increase both your policy's cash value and its death benefit, allowing you to enhance the financial security your policy offers. Over time, this increase can lead to more substantial borrowing power against your cash value for future investments or financial needs.

Compounding Growth: The beauty of compounding is that your money grows on itself. By reinvesting dividends, you benefit from growth not only on your original contributions but also on the accumulated dividends. This compounded growth creates a snowball effect, which can significantly boost the value of your policy in the long run.

Tax Advantages: Dividends reinvested within your life insurance policy typically grow tax-deferred. This tax-advantaged compounding makes reinvesting an efficient way to grow wealth without facing annual tax obligations, allowing you to retain more of your earnings.

KEY CONSIDERATIONS FOR REINVESTING

Long-Term Goals: If you're focused on wealth accumulation, legacy building, or expanding future financial flexibility, reinvesting is often advantageous.

Policy Performance: Review your insurer's historical dividend performance to understand how reinvested dividends are likely to impact your policy. Policies from financially stable insurers with strong dividend track records are generally better candidates for reinvestment.

THE CASE FOR TAKING CASH PAYOUTS

Opting for cash payouts on your dividends provides immediate financial flexibility. This approach can be especially helpful if you have current expenses to cover or other investment opportunities outside of your life insurance policy.

Immediate Liquidity: Cash payouts provide you with instant funds that you can use as you see fit. This liquidity can be directed toward expanding your business, investing in stocks, or even making a down payment on real estate.

Control Over Finances: Taking dividends as cash allows you to allocate the funds in a way that aligns with your current priorities. Whether it's reinvesting in other wealth-building avenues, covering daily expenses, or building an emergency fund, this approach lets you make the most of your life insurance policy's payout power.

Flexibility for Short-Term Goals: If you have short-term financial needs, taking cash dividends can serve as a bridge, helping you avoid additional debt or reducing the need to dip into other investments.

KEY CONSIDERATIONS FOR TAKING PAYOUTS

Current Financial Needs: If you have immediate obligations, such as covering operating expenses for your business or investing in your education, cash payouts may offer the most practical solution.

Tax Implications: While dividends are often tax-free up to the amount you've paid in premiums, exceeding that can trigger taxes. Keep this in mind if you plan to use cash payouts for wealth-building.

WEIGHING YOUR OPTIONS

Choosing between reinvesting dividends and taking cash payouts depends on your financial priorities and long-term plans. Consider the following factors when making your decision:

Are You Focusing on Wealth Accumulation? If building substantial wealth or creating a legacy is your goal, reinvesting dividends is a powerful strategy.

Do You Have Immediate Financial Needs? If you're looking to cover expenses, invest elsewhere, or fund short-term goals, taking cash payouts might better suit your needs.

Can You Manage without the Cash? Reinvesting dividends often means sacrificing short-term cash flow for long-term growth. Assess whether your finances allow for this approach without compromising your current needs.

MAKING AN INFORMED DECISION

Ensuring you're making the most of your dividends requires regular reviews and staying informed about your policy's performance. Here are some practical steps:

Schedule Regular Policy Reviews: By meeting with your insurance advisor, you can stay updated on policy performance, assess whether your current dividend strategy aligns with your goals, and adjust your approach as needed.

Consult Financial Professionals: A financial advisor can provide insight into the tax implications and potential benefits of each option, helping you make choices that fit your broader financial plan.

Stay Informed on Market Conditions: Monitoring interest rates, dividend trends, and the financial stability of your insurer can help you decide whether it's time to adjust your strategy.

CHOOSING THE RIGHT APPROACH FOR WEALTH BUILDING

Deciding whether to reinvest or take cash dividends can significantly impact your financial future. By assessing your immediate and long-term goals, you can make an informed choice that helps you leverage your life insurance policy to its fullest potential.

In the next section, we explore the various ways you can leverage your policy as collateral, allowing you to access funds for other opportunities without depleting your savings.

PART 4: LEVERAGING LIFE INSURANCE FOR LOANS AND INVESTMENTS

12: USING CASH VALUE AS COLLATERAL FOR OTHER LOANS

UNLOCKING FINANCIAL FLEXIBILITY WITH YOUR LIFE INSURANCE POLICY

Your cash value can also be used as collateral for other types of loans. By leveraging your life insurance policy's cash value as collateral, you gain access to funds while still maintaining your insurance coverage, which can prove highly advantageous.

In this chapter, we'll explore how to use cash value as collateral, the benefits it can offer, and the essential considerations you should be aware of before taking this step.

WHAT DOES IT MEAN TO USE YOUR POLICY AS COLLATERAL?

When you use your life insurance policy's cash value as collateral, you're effectively offering it as a security guarantee to the lender. Because life insurance cash value is considered an asset, it provides assurance to lenders that you have the financial backing to repay the loan.

This can increase your chances of loan approval or even enable you to qualify for a lower interest rate compared to an unsecured loan. By acting as collateral, your life insurance policy gives the lender confidence that they will be repaid, as they can claim the cash value if you default.

KEY FEATURES OF USING LIFE INSURANCE AS COLLATERAL:

Loan Security: The cash value becomes an asset that the lender can rely on, reducing their risk.

Interest Rate Benefits: Collateralized loans often come with more favorable terms, potentially including lower interest rates.

Flexibility: Using your policy as collateral can allow you to maintain liquidity in other areas of your finances while still securing the loan.

Potential for Higher Loan Amounts: With collateral backing the loan, lenders are often willing to approve larger loan amounts than they would for an unsecured loan.

WHEN TO CONSIDER USING LIFE INSURANCE AS COLLATERAL

While using life insurance as collateral can be a beneficial strategy, it's not always the right choice for everyone. Here are some scenarios where it may be particularly advantageous:

Large Purchases or Investments: If you're planning a significant investment, such as in real estate or a business venture, using life insurance as collateral can help you obtain the necessary funds without liquidating other assets.

Need for Favorable Loan Terms: If you're looking to minimize interest costs or are seeking a larger loan, the collateralization of your life insurance may help you achieve these goals.

Insufficient or Limited Other Assets: If you don't have assets like property or investments to offer as collateral, your life insurance can serve this purpose while also providing financial protection to your loved ones.

HOW IT WORKS: STEPS TO USING LIFE INSURANCE AS COL-

LATERAL

Verify Cash Value Availability: First, confirm that your life insurance policy has a cash value component. Typically, term life insurance policies do not accumulate cash value, so only certain types of permanent life insurance qualify.

Contact Your Insurer and Lender: Notify your insurance company that you plan to use your policy as collateral. Some policies have specific clauses related to collateralization, so it's essential to review any restrictions or requirements.

Submit Collateral Assignment Documents: You'll need to complete and submit a collateral assignment form. This is a legal document indicating that you are using your policy's cash value as collateral for the loan.

Evaluate Loan Terms: Once your collateral is confirmed, review the loan terms to ensure they align with your financial goals. Collateralized loans can offer various benefits, but it's critical to understand how they affect both your loan and your life insurance policy.

Monitor Policy Status: While your policy is collateralized, make sure to maintain the premium payments to keep the policy active. A lapse in payment could void the collateral assignment and potentially the loan as well.

BENEFITS OF USING LIFE INSURANCE AS COLLATERAL

There are several notable advantages to using a life insurance policy's cash value to secure a loan:

Better Loan Terms: Since the lender has collateral, you may qualify for more favorable interest rates than you would with an unsecured loan.

Preserves Other Assets: Instead of selling or liquidating other assets, such as stocks or property, you can leverage your life insurance policy, allowing you to keep other investments intact.

Retains Policy Benefits: By using the cash value rather than surrendering the policy, you continue to retain life insurance protection for your beneficiaries, which can be an invaluable form of security.

Flexible Repayment Options: Since the policy itself is not directly loaned against, you may have greater flexibility in how you repay the loan, especially if it's from a third-party lender.

ESSENTIAL CONSIDERATIONS AND RISKS

While using your life insurance policy as collateral can offer various benefits, it's crucial to consider the potential downsides and limitations:

Impact on Death Benefit: If you pass away with an outstanding loan balance, the lender will be paid first from your death benefit, reducing the amount your beneficiaries receive. This can significantly impact their financial stability, so it's essential to have a repayment plan in place.

Policy Maintenance: You must keep up with premium payments to maintain the policy's active status. A lapse could result in the loss of both the collateral value and the loan terms.

Limited Cash Value Availability: Depending on your policy's accumulated cash value, there may be a limit to how much you can use as collateral. If your cash value is lower than the loan amount you need, you may need additional sources of collateral.

Potential Opportunity Cost: When using the cash value as collateral, you're tying up a significant portion of your life insurance policy's benefit in securing a loan, which could have been allocated toward other financial goals.

PRACTICAL EXAMPLE OF USING CASH VALUE AS COLLATERAL

Consider Sarah, who has a whole life insurance policy with $100,000 in cash value. Sarah wishes to start a business and needs a loan of $50,000. By using her policy's cash value as collateral, Sarah's lender approves her for a loan with a reduced interest rate, as the policy serves as security.

This arrangement allows Sarah to avoid liquidating other assets, and as long as she makes timely payments, her life insurance policy remains intact, preserving the death benefit for her family.

If Sarah passes away before repaying the loan, the outstanding balance will be deducted from her policy's death benefit. This arrangement demonstrates the balance between leveraging cash value for financial gain and the responsibility of managing repayment to ensure her beneficiaries still benefit from the policy.

WEIGHING THE PROS AND CONS

Using your life insurance policy's cash value as collateral is a strategic financial decision. It offers access to funds with the added security of better loan terms and preserves other assets. However, it's essential to recognize the potential reduction in your death benefit and the importance of maintaining the policy.

Leveraging your life insurance policy's cash value as collateral can unlock opportunities for larger, lower-cost loans. It's an option that can serve well when used strategically, especially for those looking to finance investments or business ventures.

In the next chapter, we'll explore additional ways to maximize your policy's cash value through policy loans and creative financing methods, helping you build financial flexibility with the resources at your disposal.

13: FUNDING OTHER INVESTMENTS WITH LOANS

UNLOCKING OPPORTUNITIES THROUGH STRATEGIC BORROWING

U sing your life insurance policy's cash value as collateral for loans can open up a range of investment opportunities. By tapping into these funds, you can leverage your existing assets to grow your wealth further. In this chapter, we'll explore how to use life insurance-backed loans for investing, the types of investments to consider, and the key considerations to keep in mind.

INVESTMENT OPPORTUNITIES

Leveraging your life insurance policy's cash value can open doors to diverse investment opportunities, providing a strategic path to grow your wealth. Here are several effective ways to put these funds to work:

Real Estate: Using a life insurance-backed loan for real estate investments is a popular strategy. Whether you're purchasing rental properties, flipping homes, or investing in commercial real estate, this approach can help generate a steady income stream.

Real estate often appreciates over time, adding value to your portfolio and offering potential returns that can cover or exceed your loan interest costs.

Growing Your Business or Side Hustle: Whether you're scaling your current business or boosting your side hustle, cash value from your life insurance policy offers low-interest capital to fuel growth. This investment can help fund inventory, increase marketing efforts, or expand operations, ultimately increasing revenue.

By investing in growth, you can create a cycle of reinvestment and profitability, enhancing your business's income potential.

Investing in Forex: The Forex market offers a unique investment avenue for life insurance-backed loans. Rather than trading currencies yourself, you can have professional Forex traders manage your funds. These experts can strategically trade on your behalf, capitalizing on currency fluctuations for profit.

Although the Forex market can be volatile, an experienced trader can help navigate these risks, potentially delivering returns that exceed the cost of your loan.

Stock Market Investments: If you're familiar with stock market investing, these funds can help expand your stock portfolio. By selecting stocks, ETFs, or mutual funds with solid growth potential, you may be able to yield high returns that exceed the loan's interest rate. It's essential to research and diversify carefully, as the market can be volatile. With careful planning, you can strategically manage risks while potentially multiplying your investment.

Using your life insurance's cash value for income-generating investments can provide flexible, low-cost capital that maximizes growth potential. However, each option carries its own risks, so careful evaluation and alignment with your financial goals are essential for maximizing the benefits.

BENEFITS OF INVESTING WITH POLICY LOANS

Leverage Existing Assets: By using your life insurance policy's cash value, you can leverage existing assets to make new investments without liquidating other investments or savings. This strategic approach allows you to maintain your financial portfolio while pursuing new opportunities.

Tax Advantages: The interest on a life insurance-backed loan may be tax-deductible, depending on how you use the funds and your tax situation. Additionally, the cash value growth of your life insurance policy is tax-deferred, providing an added layer of tax efficiency.

Increased Financial Flexibility: Utilizing life insurance-backed loans can enhance your overall financial flexibility. You can adjust your repayment strategy based on your cash flow, allowing you to manage your investments and personal finances more effectively.

KEY CONSIDERATIONS

Risk Assessment: While funding investments with life insurance-backed loans can be beneficial, it's crucial to assess the associated risks. If the investments do not perform as expected, you could face difficulties in repaying the loan, which may jeopardize your policy's death benefit.

Maintaining Adequate Cash Value: Ensure that your policy maintains sufficient cash value to cover the loan balance and any interest accrued. If the loan amount exceeds the cash value, it can lead to policy lapse, which could have serious financial consequences.

Long-Term Financial Planning: Incorporating life insurance-backed loans into your investment strategy requires careful long-term financial planning. Consider your overall financial goals, risk tolerance, and how these investments align with your broader objectives.

A STRATEGIC INVESTMENT APPROACH

Leveraging your life insurance policy for funding investments can unlock significant financial opportunities. By strategically using these loans, you can pursue various avenues for growth while maintaining financial stability.

In the chapters that follow, you'll find a roadmap for making the most of your life insurance policy as a funding tool, empowering you to pursue diverse investments and enhance your wealth-building strategy.

14: BUILDING A REAL ESTATE PORTFOLIO

LEVERAGING CASH VALUE TO FINANCE PROPERTY INVESTMENTS

For investors looking to build a real estate portfolio, leveraging the cash value of a life insurance policy can be an accessible and strategic way to obtain funding. By using the accumulated cash value as collateral, you gain access to funds that can be invested in rental properties or other real estate opportunities.

This approach not only preserves your policy's death benefit but also provides a lower-interest borrowing option that can support steady portfolio growth.

WHY REAL ESTATE?

Real estate investing offers unique advantages, such as steady income, potential property appreciation, and tax benefits. Unlike stocks or bonds, real estate assets are tangible and, with the right management, can appreciate consistently over time. Rental properties, in particular, create a passive income stream that can supplement or even replace earned income, making real estate an appealing choice for wealth building.

UNDERSTANDING LEVERAGE: BORROWING TO INVEST

Leverage is a fundamental concept in real estate investment. By borrowing funds to purchase properties, you can acquire assets with only a fraction of their cost upfront. The idea is to invest other people's money, typically through mortgages or loans, to acquire properties that appreciate over time, thus amplifying your returns. For example, if you buy a rental property with a mortgage, the property's rental income can cover the loan payments while still leaving a profit.

However, using leverage requires careful planning to ensure loan payments are manageable and do not outweigh rental income.

WHY USE CASH VALUE AS COLLATERAL FOR REAL ESTATE INVESTMENTS?

Borrowing against your cash value allows you to access funds without withdrawing or surrendering the policy, keeping your insurance coverage intact while opening the door to investment opportunities. Using a life insurance policy loan often comes with lower interest rates than traditional loans, especially if you have a permanent life insurance policy that has built substantial cash value over time.

When invested wisely in real estate, these borrowed funds can yield returns greater than the loan's interest rate, making it a financially smart move.

UNDERSTANDING POLICY LOANS FOR REAL ESTATE INVESTMENTS

A cash value loan is essentially an advance on your death benefit, and unlike a mortgage or personal loan, repayment terms are flexible. This flexibility allows you to tailor repayment to align with your real estate income, reinvesting property profits back into the policy loan to reduce debt while still benefiting from rental income.

When borrowing for real estate investments, keep these key

points in mind:

Interest Costs vs. Property Returns: The goal is to invest in properties that will yield returns above the loan interest rate. This positive spread can create a profitable investment cycle, where rental income and property appreciation work to grow your wealth.

Properties in high-demand areas with strong rental markets are ideal, as they are more likely to yield steady income that covers loan payments and generates profit.

Policy Loan Impact on Death Benefit: Outstanding loans reduce the death benefit, so it's important to ensure that you're either repaying the loan or generating enough from your investments to cover any loan balance over time.

CHOOSING THE RIGHT PROPERTIES

Real estate investments are most profitable when they offer solid cash flow and long-term appreciation. With your policy loan funding, you can strategically enter the real estate market by selecting properties that align with these goals. Consider these tips:

Location: Target high-demand rental markets. Look for areas with low vacancy rates and strong rental demand. Properties in growing neighborhoods or near schools, public transport, and employment hubs often command higher rents and appreciate faster.

Property Type and Size: Evaluate multi-unit properties. Multi-family units provide multiple streams of rental income, which can boost your return on investment and help cover loan repayment. They also diversify rental risk, as vacancies in one unit are offset by occupancy in others.

Condition and Upkeep Costs: Older properties may require extensive renovations, while newer ones might have lower upkeep costs. Always factor in any repair or improvement expenses to ensure you're not exceeding your budget.

USING CASH FLOW TO MANAGE LOAN REPAYMENT

Rental income from your real estate properties can be a natural source of cash flow to cover policy loan interest and principal. As you manage your properties, aim to structure your cash flow as follows:

Set Aside Funds for Loan Repayment: Allocate a portion of rental income specifically toward repaying your policy loan, ensuring that your loan balance decreases over time.

Build a Reserve Fund: Keep a portion of profits in reserve for property maintenance and unexpected expenses. This approach preserves rental income and prevents cash flow interruptions that could impact your ability to service the loan.

FINANCING OPTIONS WITH CASH VALUE LOANS

As you scale your real estate investments, consider how cash value loans can provide initial capital or bridge financing. They can be particularly useful when you want to:

Cover Down Payments: Use the loan as a down payment, securing conventional financing to fund the remaining property purchase. This hybrid approach lets you invest in larger properties without depleting your cash flow.

Fund Property Renovations: Improve property value by using a policy loan for renovations or upgrades, which can justify higher rent and enhance property value over time.

MANAGING YOUR PORTFOLIO

Effective property management is essential for maintaining steady income and tenant satisfaction. As you build your portfolio, consider these management tips:

Screen Tenants Carefully: Vetting tenants ensures you choose reliable renters who pay on time and take care of the property.

Set Competitive Rent Rates: Analyze local rental rates to set competitive yet profitable rents that attract tenants quickly.

Keep Up with Maintenance: Regular maintenance prevents costly repairs and keeps properties attractive to renters.

For larger portfolios, you may want to work with a property management company to handle tenant relations, repairs, and rent collection, freeing you up to focus on strategic growth.

SCALING YOUR PORTFOLIO

Expanding your real estate portfolio is a long-term commitment. Consider these strategies for scaling:

Reinvest Profits: Use rental income to fund new investments, gradually expanding your holdings without excessive borrowing.

Utilize Refinancing: Refinancing properties at lower interest rates or cashing out equity can provide funds for additional purchases.

Diversify Locations and Property Types: Diversifying helps manage risk by spreading investments across different markets and property types, reducing vulnerability to local market fluctuations.

By reinvesting and refinancing strategically, you can expand your real estate portfolio over time, maximizing the wealth-generating potential of your assets.

EXAMPLE: INVESTING IN A RENTAL PROPERTY WITH CASH VALUE AS COLLATERAL

Background: Sarah has accumulated a significant cash value in her whole life insurance policy. She's interested in building a real estate portfolio and has found a promising rental property valued at $200,000. Her goal is to generate passive income through rental payments and to benefit from property appreciation over time.

Transaction Setup:

Down Payment: 20% of $200,000, or $40,000

Loan Type: Traditional mortgage covering 80% of the property value, or $160,000

Cash Value Loan: Sarah borrows $40,000 against her policy's cash value as collateral to cover the down payment. The loan has an interest rate of 5%, and repayment terms are flexible, allowing her to decide how quickly she wants to repay it.

Projected Income and Expenses

- **Monthly Rent**: $1,500
- **Mortgage Payment (Principal + Interest)**: $850/month
- **Property Management, Maintenance, and Taxes**: $250/month
- **Cash Flow**: $1,500 - ($850 + $250) = $400/month in positive cash flow

Total Returns

Cash Flow: Sarah earns approximately $400/month in net rental income, totaling $4,800 annually.

Property Appreciation: Assuming the property appreciates by 5% per year, it could be worth about $220,000 in two years, giving her an additional $20,000 in equity.

Policy Loan: The interest Sarah pays on her $40,000 loan (if she doesn't repay it immediately) is outweighed by her rental income, allowing her to cover the loan costs while generating positive cash flow.

Profit Summary After 2 Years

- **Total Rental Income**: $9,600
- **Property Appreciation**: $20,000 in estimated equity gain
- **Total Value Growth**: $29,600

By leveraging her cash value, Sarah could successfully enter the real estate market and build her portfolio without needing out-of-pocket cash for the down payment, making this a profitable transaction by generating rental income and building equity.

Sarah has several options for repaying her cash value loan from the insurance policy, each with its own financial impact. Here's how she can manage it effectively:

1. Using Monthly Rental Income

Sarah earns $400 per month in positive cash flow from her rental property. She could allocate a portion or the entirety of this income toward repaying her cash value loan. She could also make lump sum payments from other sources to pay down the loan at a faster rate.

2. Flexible Repayment Over Time

Cash value loans from life insurance policies are typically flexible, meaning there's no fixed repayment schedule. If Sarah wants to maximize cash flow, she could prioritize reinvesting rental income into other properties or assets and defer paying down the policy loan, as long as she manages any accrued interest.

By using these strategies, Sarah has the flexibility to balance her loan repayment with her investment goals, ensuring she maintains both liquidity and growth potential in her real estate portfolio.

Building a real estate portfolio by leveraging cash value from your life insurance policy offers a strategic approach to wealth generation. By using your policy as collateral, you gain access to lower-cost funding that allows you to capitalize on real estate opportunities without sacrificing your insurance benefits.

With a disciplined approach to loan repayment and property selection, you can use this strategy to grow a real estate portfolio that enhances your financial future while preserving your life insurance coverage.

15: GROWING YOUR BUSINESS
A FLEXIBLE FUNDING STRATEGY FOR ENTREPRENEURS

L ife insurance-backed loans can provide a powerful source of funding for entrepreneurs and business owners seeking to grow or expand their ventures. By borrowing against the cash value within your life insurance policy, you gain access to a flexible financing source that can help you achieve your business goals without the stringent requirements or high interest rates associated with traditional bank loans.

This chapter delves into practical ways to use cash value loans to support business development, manage loan repayment effectively, and ensure that both your business and financial future thrive.

WHY USE A LIFE INSURANCE LOAN TO GROW YOUR BUSINESS?

Using a cash value loan to fund your business growth has several advantages:

Lower Interest Rates: Life insurance loans typically offer competitive rates, making it easier to keep loan costs manageable.

Flexible Repayment: Unlike bank loans with fixed schedules, life insurance loans offer flexibility in how and when you repay, allowing you to align repayments with your business cash flow.

Preserving Equity: By using a life insurance loan instead of seeking external investors, you retain full control and ownership of your business.

For entrepreneurs who want to start a new side hustle or small business, the lower barrier to entry provided by a life insurance loan can be a game-changer.

STRATEGIES FOR FUNDING BUSINESS GROWTH WITH CASH VALUE LOANS

Cash value loans are versatile, and there are many ways to apply them within your business to achieve profitable growth. Here are some approaches to consider:

Expanding Inventory: If demand is growing, using your life insurance loan to increase inventory can help you meet customer needs without delay, potentially boosting sales and building a loyal customer base.

Investing in Marketing and Advertising: Marketing can play a crucial role in a business's growth trajectory. A well-funded marketing campaign can increase brand awareness, drive traffic to your website or store, and ultimately improve your revenue. Using cash value for advertising allows you to strategically scale your outreach without tapping into operating revenue.

Upgrading Technology and Equipment: Using your policy loan to fund essential upgrades, like new software, updated machinery, or customer relationship management tools, can help your business operate more efficiently. These investments, although costly, often pay for themselves over time as they streamline processes and reduce overhead costs.

Hiring New Staff: Growing your team can be essential to meet demand and improve customer service. With cash from your life insurance loan, you can onboard additional talent, whether they're in sales, customer support, or operations, to build a stronger foundation for your business.

Example: Funding a New Side Hustle Using Cash Value Loans

Suppose you've been operating a part-time consulting business and see an opportunity to go full-time. With your current savings tied up, you turn to your life insurance cash value to cover startup costs. Using a cash value loan to launch a small office, invest in marketing, and purchase necessary equipment allows you to grow your consulting business without the pressure of high-interest debt or giving up equity.

MANAGING REPAYMENT TO PROTECT POLICY BENEFITS

Repaying your life insurance loan is vital to maintaining the policy's long-term value and preserving the death benefit for your beneficiaries. Here's how to manage repayment effectively:

Plan for Incremental Repayments: While repayments on life insurance loans are flexible, setting up an incremental repayment schedule can prevent the loan balance from growing due to accrued interest.

Utilize Business Revenue: As your business begins to grow and generate revenue, allocate a portion to repaying the loan. By applying profits toward the loan, you can gradually reduce the balance while preserving the health of your life insurance policy.

Reinvest Wisely: Any additional profits or cash flow generated from your business can be reinvested to reduce the loan balance faster, enabling you to benefit from both business growth and the ongoing value of your policy.

ENSURING FUTURE FINANCIAL SECURITY

Leveraging life insurance loans for business growth can be a strategic financial decision, but it's essential to weigh the impacts. Understand that while a policy loan is a low-cost, flexible borrowing option, any outstanding balance will reduce the death benefit available to your beneficiaries if not fully repaid. Balancing growth and repayment is critical to ensure that your business prospers without jeopardizing the long-term security that life insurance provides.

Growing your business with a life insurance loan is a valuable strategy for entrepreneurs who seek to expand without tapping into high-interest debt or giving up ownership equity. By thoughtfully applying cash value loans to strategic business needs and managing repayment, you create a dual advantage—fueling your entrepreneurial ambitions while protecting your financial future.

Whether you're growing a side hustle or scaling a full-fledged business, this chapter illustrates how life insurance can be a smart partner in your business success journey.

16: FUNDING FOREX INVESTMENT

FUNDING STRATEGY FOR FOREX PASSIVE INCOME

L everaging life insurance loans to fund a Forex investment strategy can be a powerful approach for generating passive income without needing to trade directly. Instead of engaging in high-risk, hands-on trading yourself, you can use the cash value from your life insurance policy to fund skilled, experienced Forex traders.

By working with traders who understand the market and operate with strategic discipline, you can put your policy's funds to work, aiming for returns that exceed the loan's interest rate.

Here's a breakdown of how funding a Forex investment works, including the risks, potential rewards, and steps to set up a profitable partnership with a professional Forex trader or fund:

UNDERSTANDING FOREX AS AN INVESTMENT TOOL

What is Forex Trading?: Forex, or foreign exchange, involves buying and selling currency pairs, like EUR/USD, to profit from exchange rate fluctuations. This market operates 24/7 and is known for its high liquidity.

Why Work with Professionals?: Forex requires expertise, quick responses to market changes, and understanding of global economic factors. By partnering with a Forex professional or managed account service, you rely on a trader's experience to navigate this volatile market on your behalf.

SETTING UP A LIFE INSURANCE LOAN FOR FOREX FUNDING

Using Your Policy as Collateral: Once you've built up enough cash value in your policy, you can borrow against it to invest in Forex. The loan is typically secured against your cash value, allowing you to access funds without tapping into personal savings.

Interest and Repayment: Life insurance loans offer relatively low-interest rates and flexible repayment options. As long as your Forex investment generates a return above the loan's interest rate, you could potentially achieve positive cash flow.

STEPS TO PARTNER WITH A FOREX PROFESSIONAL

Research Reputable Traders or Funds: Look for professional traders or Forex funds with a track record of consistent returns. Online reviews, performance metrics, and testimonials from other investors can be helpful in making a decision.

Evaluate Risk Management: Ensure that your chosen Forex professional employs strategies that manage risk effectively, as Forex is a volatile market. Traders who use tools like stop-loss orders, diversification, and hedging may offer more stability in returns.

Define Terms and Expectations: Discuss the terms of your investment, such as potential returns, fees, and how frequently you'll receive updates on your account performance.

ANALYZING PROFIT POTENTIAL AND RISKS

Calculating Potential Gains: Estimate the profit margin by comparing the trader's historical returns with your loan interest rate. For example, if your loan rate is 5% and the trader's annual returns average around 10-15%, you may achieve a net gain of

5-10%.

Mitigating Risks: Forex investments can be high-risk, so be prepared for fluctuations. Diversifying your investments and limiting the amount borrowed can help reduce exposure to sudden market shifts.

MONITORING AND ADJUSTING YOUR INVESTMENT

Track Performance Regularly: Review monthly or quarterly reports from your Forex professional to stay informed on gains or losses.

Plan for Loan Repayment: Regularly assess whether to reinvest returns or use them to pay down your life insurance loan. This keeps your overall debt low while allowing you to retain control over investment earnings.

BALANCING RETURNS WITH LOAN REPAYMENT GOALS

Strategic Loan Repayment: If your Forex returns are performing well, consider using a portion of the earnings to pay down your loan. Alternatively, reinvest if the market shows growth potential.

Revisiting Your Strategy: As your cash value grows and your knowledge of Forex deepens, reassess your financial strategy to ensure alignment with your income goals.

By leveraging your life insurance cash value to fund professional Forex investments, you can access a new stream of potential passive income. However, like any investment, thorough research, clear objectives, and regular oversight are critical to maximizing the value of this strategy while protecting your policy's cash value and the benefits it provides.

In the next chapter, we'll focus on the need to build a strong foundation through education, as informed investing makes the difference between merely funding an opportunity and creating lasting financial growth.

17: INVEST IN YOUR EDUCATION BEFORE INVESTING

EMPOWER YOUR INVESTMENT JOURNEY THROUGH KNOWLEDGE

Before diving into any investment opportunity—whether it's building a real estate portfolio, expanding your business, or funding your forex investments—it's crucial to prioritize your education. Understanding the nuances of each investment avenue can be the difference between success and failure.

BUILDING A REAL ESTATE PORTFOLIO

Investing in real estate can be lucrative, but it's essential to grasp the fundamentals of the market. Begin by learning about property valuation, which involves understanding how to determine the worth of a property based on various factors, including location, size, and condition. Familiarize yourself with rental income analysis, which requires knowledge of market rents, vacancy rates, and operating expenses to accurately assess potential cash flow.

Equally important are the local laws and regulations that govern real estate transactions. These can include zoning laws, tenant rights, and property taxes, which vary by jurisdiction. Educating yourself on these aspects not only helps you avoid legal pitfalls but also empowers you to negotiate better deals and understand the implications of your investments.

Consider taking formal courses, attending seminars, or connecting with experienced investors who can share their insights. Networking with real estate professionals can provide you with mentorship opportunities and access to resources that enhance your learning experience. The more informed you are about the real estate market, the more confident you'll be in making decisions on when to buy, hold, or sell properties.

GROWING YOUR BUSINESS

Whether you're starting a side hustle or looking to scale an existing business, having a solid understanding of business fundamentals is key. This includes mastering marketing strategies to effectively reach your target audience, managing finances to ensure sustainability, and developing strong customer relations to build loyalty.

Investing in your education can help you identify market gaps where your business can thrive. For instance, learning about digital marketing can equip you with the tools to promote your business online, while courses in financial management can teach you how to budget and allocate resources efficiently.

Resources such as online courses, business workshops, and mentorship programs can be invaluable. These platforms provide opportunities to learn from industry experts and gain practical experience. Engaging with fellow entrepreneurs can also foster collaboration and lead to valuable partnerships that drive growth. The more knowledgeable you become about the intricacies of running a business, the better positioned you'll be to navigate challenges and seize opportunities.

FUNDING FOREX INVESTMENTS

In the realm of funding forex investments, it's essential to comprehend the nuances of this dynamic market, especially if you're not a trader yourself. Forex trading can appear intimidating, with its myriad of strategies and constant market fluctuations. However, educating yourself on the fundamental principles of forex investing is crucial, particularly if you plan to have professional traders manage your investments.

Start by learning about key concepts such as currency pairs, pips, and leverage. Understanding how these elements interact can help you make informed decisions regarding your investments. Familiarize yourself with the strategies employed by successful traders, such as technical analysis, which involves analyzing price charts, and fundamental analysis, which looks at economic indicators and news events that impact currency values.

Moreover, grasping the factors influencing currency movements —like geopolitical events, economic data releases, and market sentiment—can enhance your ability to communicate effectively with your investment managers. By being well-versed in forex principles, you can engage in meaningful discussions about your portfolio's performance and adjust your investment strategies as needed.

By investing in your education across these three areas, you position yourself for better outcomes and increase your chances of achieving your financial goals. Remember, the more informed you are, the better equipped you'll be to make strategic investments that align with your overall wealth-building strategy.

Education is a powerful tool that empowers you to make confident decisions and seize opportunities across various investment avenues. Whether you're navigating the complexities of real estate, the challenges of entrepreneurship, or the intricacies of forex investing, a commitment to learning can set you on a path toward sustainable financial success.

In the next section, we'll look at common mistakes people make when leveraging their life insurance for investments, such as overborrowing, neglecting loan payments, or underestimating tax implications.

PART 5: COMMON PITFALLS TO AVOID

18: AVOIDING COSTLY MISTAKES WHEN BORROWING

PROTECTING YOUR WEALTH BY UNDERSTANDING THE RISKS

Borrowing against your life insurance policy can unlock valuable cash that can be used for various purposes, from funding investments to covering unexpected expenses. However, this strategy comes with potential risks. Knowing the pitfalls and avoiding common mistakes can help you make the most of your life insurance policy without jeopardizing your long-term financial goals. This chapter will guide you through key mistakes to avoid when leveraging your life insurance for cash.

**BORROWING AGAINST YOUR POLICY:
WHAT TO WATCH OUT FOR**

Taking on Excessive Loans: One of the most common mistakes policyholders make is borrowing too much against their policy's cash value. While it may be tempting to access a larger sum, excessive borrowing can create significant financial strain if you're unable to repay the loan. This not only depletes the cash value but can also reduce the death benefit your beneficiaries would receive. In extreme cases, it can even lead to a policy lapse, which means losing both your coverage and any remaining cash value.

Ignoring Loan Interest Payments: When you borrow against your policy, interest is charged on the outstanding loan balance. It's critical to keep track of these interest payments, as neglecting them can result in the loan amount growing over time. Unpaid interest accumulates, leaving you with a larger loan balance than anticipated and diminishing the cash value of your policy faster than expected.

Risk of Policy Lapse: Another significant risk of borrowing against your life insurance policy is the potential for a policy lapse. If loans are left unpaid or if the total loans exceed the cash value, the policy can lapse, resulting in the termination of coverage and the loss of any cash value. This not only means losing important insurance protection but can also have tax implications, particularly if you have taken substantial loans against the policy.

COMMON BORROWING MISTAKES TO AVOID

Failing to Account for Policy Fees: When borrowing against your policy, be mindful of any fees that may be associated with the loan. Some insurance policies come with administrative costs that can reduce the actual cash you receive. Understanding these fees upfront helps you make informed decisions and avoid unexpected surprises.

Missing the Fine Print on Policy Loans: Each insurance company has different rules regarding loan repayment, interest rates, and policies on unpaid loans. Familiarizing yourself with the specifics of your policy is crucial to avoid unintentional breaches, which could lead to policy cancellation or higher interest costs.

Borrowing Without Exploring Alternatives: While borrowing against your life insurance can provide immediate cash, it's essential to explore all available options before proceeding. Alternatives such as partial withdrawals, other lines of credit, or personal savings might provide the funds you need without compromising your policy's long-term benefits. Consulting with a financial advisor can help you choose the most suitable strategy.

STRATEGIES TO AVOID FINANCIAL PITFALLS

Maintaining a Low Loan Balance: To minimize the risk of policy lapse and maintain policy value, it's best to borrow conservatively. By keeping loan amounts low and making regular payments, you can preserve both cash value and death benefits for future use. This proactive approach can provide a safety net for unforeseen expenses while keeping your insurance policy intact.

Staying on Top of Interest Payments: Even if you can't pay back the entire loan immediately, ensuring that you cover interest payments is vital. This practice helps to control the loan balance and prevents compounding interest from eroding the cash value. It also reduces the risk of policy lapse, allowing you to maintain your coverage while managing your loan effectively.

Consulting with a Financial Professional: Borrowing against a life insurance policy is a significant decision with long-term consequences. Working with a financial advisor can provide clarity, help you avoid costly mistakes, and ensure your actions align with your overall financial goals. An advisor can help you navigate the intricacies of your policy and develop a comprehensive strategy for borrowing that minimizes risks.

Requesting a Policy Loan Illustration: Most insurance companies can provide a loan illustration showing how different loan amounts and interest payments will affect your policy over time. This visual tool can help you plan and decide on a sustainable borrowing amount. By understanding the long-term implications of your borrowing decisions, you can make informed choices that support your financial well-being.

MAKING INFORMED CHOICES FOR FINANCIAL SECURITY

Accessing cash through life insurance policy loans can be beneficial, but it requires caution and planning. By avoiding common pitfalls and being aware of the risks involved, you can make informed decisions that provide immediate funds without compromising your long-term financial security.

In the next chapter, we'll address the importance of understanding the fine print in your life insurance policy.

19: AVOIDING HIDDEN FEES IN POLICY TERMS

DECODING LIFE INSURANCE LANGUAGE

L ife insurance policies come with many terms, conditions, and fees that can impact the policy's long-term value. Knowing how to interpret these terms helps you avoid hidden costs and make the most of your policy's income potential. In this chapter, we'll go through common policy terms, explain how fees work, and provide guidance on how to keep costs low to protect your wealth.

COMMON POLICY FEES AND HOW THEY AFFECT YOU

Administrative Fees: Administrative fees are standard with most life insurance policies and cover the costs of maintaining your policy. These fees may seem small, but over the years, they can add up and reduce the policy's cash value and potential earnings.

Mortality and Expense (M&E) Fees: M&E fees are charges for covering the cost of insuring the policyholder. They're typically calculated based on the amount of coverage or death benefit and are deducted regularly from the policy's cash value. Understanding how much you're paying in M&E fees can help you gauge whether the policy is cost-effective over time.

Surrender Charges: If you decide to terminate your policy within a certain period, a surrender charge applies. Surrender periods vary, but these fees can be significant during the early years of a policy. Knowing the surrender period and charges allows you to make informed decisions about policy termination.

DECODING POLICY TERMS TO AVOID SURPRISES

Premium Loads: Some policies include premium loads, which are upfront charges deducted from each premium payment. These fees reduce the amount going into the policy's cash value, which can affect growth over time. Look for policies with lower or no premium loads if cash value accumulation is important to you.

Loan Interest Rates and Conditions: If you plan to borrow against your policy, be sure to review the loan interest rates and conditions. Policies may offer fixed or variable rates, and interest payments can compound if left unpaid. Understanding how loan interest impacts the policy's cash value is essential to avoid unplanned debt.

Cash Value Growth Terms: Policies like whole and universal life have different methods for calculating cash value growth. Some policies offer a fixed growth rate, while others may tie growth to an investment index. Understanding the cash value accumulation method helps you anticipate growth and maximize earnings.

Cost of Insurance (COI) Charges: COI charges are deducted from the cash value to cover the policy's death benefit. These costs often increase with age, reducing the cash value available. Knowing how COI charges affect your policy's cash value helps you plan for future financial needs.

SPECIAL RIDERS AND HIDDEN COSTS

Accelerated Death Benefit Riders: An accelerated death benefit rider lets you access part of your death benefit while you're still alive, often in cases of terminal illness. While useful, these payouts may reduce the overall benefit available to beneficiaries and come with associated costs.

Waiver of Premium Riders: This rider covers premiums if you become disabled and are unable to work. While valuable, this rider can increase premium costs. Understanding the cost-benefit balance helps you decide if it's worth including in your policy.

Long-Term Care (LTC) Riders: LTC riders provide funds for long-term care expenses, but they usually come with additional fees that can impact cash value and benefits. Evaluating the fees for LTC riders helps ensure they align with your financial priorities.

TIPS FOR MINIMIZING FEES AND PROTECTING YOUR CASH VALUE

Shop Around for Transparent Fee Structures: Comparing policies from different insurers can help you find options with lower fees. Some insurers offer more transparent fee structures that make it easier to see how much you're paying and what value you're receiving.

Avoid Unnecessary Riders: Riders can enhance your policy, but they also increase costs. Consider whether each rider aligns with your financial goals before adding it. For example, if you don't foresee needing long-term care coverage, an LTC rider might not be necessary.

Pay Premiums Annually to Avoid Extra Charges: Some policies charge additional fees for monthly or quarterly premium payments. Paying premiums annually, if feasible, can reduce these added costs, leaving more funds for cash value growth.

Regularly Review Your Policy Statements: Regular reviews help you stay aware of fees deducted from your policy. Annual or semi-annual statements provide insight into how much you're paying in fees and whether your policy is meeting expectations.

COMMON TERMS TO KNOW FOR LONG-TERM POLICY MANAGEMENT

"Guaranteed" vs. "Non-Guaranteed" Values: Policies often distinguish between guaranteed and non-guaranteed cash values. Guaranteed values are based on fixed terms, while non-guaranteed values depend on market conditions or insurer performance. Understanding these terms helps manage expectations for future returns.

Understanding the Fine Print on Withdrawals: Policies may allow you to withdraw cash value, but some restrict the amount or frequency of withdrawals. These limits can impact how you use your policy for income generation, so understanding withdrawal terms is crucial.

Familiarity with "Indexed" Terms in Universal Life Policies: Indexed universal life policies are tied to market indices, such as the S&P 500. Knowing the index terms in your policy helps you anticipate growth and understand any associated fees, such as participation or cap rates.

GETTING EXPERT GUIDANCE TO AVOID FEE-RELATED PITFALLS

Consulting a Financial Advisor: A knowledgeable advisor can help you analyze your policy's fees and terms, allowing you to make informed decisions. They can also recommend policies with favorable fee structures suited to your goals.

Requesting Policy Illustrations: Many insurers provide policy illustrations that show fee impacts on cash value over time. Requesting an illustration offers a clear picture of your policy's potential and highlights where fees may affect future growth.

Understanding Policy Performance Reviews: Insurers often provide policy performance reviews, which give a periodic snapshot of cash value growth and fees. Reviewing these documents keeps you aware of any shifts in your policy's performance.

AVOIDING COSTLY FEES TO MAXIMIZE RETURNS

Understanding life insurance policy terms and fees empowers you to make the most of your investment. By choosing policies with transparent fees, regularly reviewing policy statements, and staying aware of hidden costs, you can reduce financial strain and maximize your returns.

In the next chapter, we'll discuss how to prevent policy lapses and protect the cash value and benefits you've worked to build. Avoiding these potential pitfalls will help you stay on track and keep your policy aligned with your income goals.

20: UNDERSTANDING POLICY LAPSES AND FINANCIAL RISKS

PROTECTING YOUR HARD-EARNED VALUE

O ne of the biggest setbacks in life insurance planning is a policy lapse. When a life insurance policy lapses, it terminates, meaning you lose all its benefits, including the death benefit, cash value, and other features that may have taken years to build. Lapses can occur due to missed premium payments or depleted cash value.

In this chapter, we'll explore what causes policy lapses, the financial impacts of letting a policy lapse, and how to avoid them to keep your income-generating strategies intact.

WHAT CAUSES A POLICY LAPSE?

Missed Premium Payments: The most common reason for a policy lapse is missed premium payments. When premiums go unpaid for a specific period, the insurance company cancels the policy. For term policies, missing a payment is typically a straightforward cancellation, but for cash value policies, lapses can be more complicated.

Depletion of Cash Value in Permanent Policies: In permanent life insurance policies like whole life or universal life, unpaid premiums can be deducted from the cash value, allowing the policy to continue without immediate payment. However, if the cash value depletes, the policy will lapse if no further payments are made. Many policyholders don't realize their cash value is at risk when they stop making payments, assuming the policy is "self-sustaining."

Policy Loan Debt: When borrowing against the cash value of a life insurance policy, interest on the loan can accumulate. If unpaid, this interest eats into the cash value, leading to potential lapses when the loan balance and interest exceed the remaining cash value. Keeping track of loan interest and repayments is key to avoiding an unplanned lapse.

FINANCIAL CONSEQUENCES OF A POLICY LAPSE

Loss of Accumulated Cash Value: In a permanent life insurance policy, years of premium payments contribute to a cash value, which is lost when a policy lapses. This forfeits both the accumulated savings and any income-generating potential, impacting your long-term financial plans.

Surrender Charges and Penalties: Some policies, particularly in the early years, have surrender charges. When a policy lapses, you may lose part of the cash value to these charges, further reducing your financial gains. Understanding your policy's surrender charge period can help you make informed decisions if lapsing becomes unavoidable.

Potential Tax Consequences: When a life insurance policy lapses, there can be tax implications, particularly if the cash value exceeds the amount of premiums paid. Any gains in the cash value may be subject to taxes, turning what seemed like a tax-advantaged account into a tax liability.

Loss of Death Benefit: If the policyholder passes away after a lapse, beneficiaries won't receive a death benefit, even if years of premiums have been paid. This can be devastating for families relying on that benefit as part of their financial planning.

HOW TO AVOID POLICY LAPSES

Set Up Automatic Premium Payments: Automatic payments reduce the risk of missed premiums. Many insurers allow you to set up autopay from your bank account, ensuring timely payments and keeping the policy active.

Monitor Your Cash Value Regularly: For policies with cash value, regular monitoring helps you stay aware of any decreases that could threaten the policy's viability. Tracking your cash value also ensures you don't accidentally deplete it by covering premiums or loan interest.

Communicate with Your Insurer: Many insurers offer grace periods before a policy officially lapses, giving you time to make missed payments and reinstate the policy. If you face financial difficulties, contact your insurer to discuss payment options or temporary adjustments.

Policy Loan Repayment Plans: If you have a policy loan, setting up a repayment plan minimizes the chance that accrued interest will eat into your cash value and cause a lapse. Even small monthly payments can help keep your loan balance under control, protecting your policy's longevity.

Review Policy Terms for Grace Periods and Reinstatement Options: Most policies include a grace period (typically 30 days) for overdue payments. After a lapse, some insurers also offer reinstatement options within a certain timeframe. Familiarizing yourself with these terms can provide a safety net in case of missed payments.

REINSTATING A LAPSED POLICY: STEPS AND CONSIDERATIONS

Contacting Your Insurer Promptly: The first step to reinstating a lapsed policy is contacting your insurance provider as soon as possible. The quicker you act, the easier it may be to reinstate without undergoing a new underwriting process.

Reinstatement Fees and Requirements: Reinstating a policy often requires paying back missed premiums, possibly with interest. Some insurers may also ask for additional underwriting, such as a health check, especially if significant time has passed since the lapse.

Evaluating If Reinstatement Is the Best Option: In some cases, reinstating an old policy might not be the best choice, especially if the fees or updated health assessments make it costly. Discussing options with a financial advisor can help you decide whether reinstatement or purchasing a new policy aligns with your goals.

TIPS FOR PROACTIVELY MANAGING YOUR POLICY

Annual Policy Reviews: Reviewing your policy annually allows you to stay aware of cash value, policy loan balances, and premium costs. Regular check-ins can help you spot potential issues before they lead to a lapse.

Adjusting Premium Payments When Needed: If premiums become unaffordable, consider adjusting the policy's payment schedule or converting to a more affordable policy type. Some permanent policies offer reduced paid-up options, where you retain a smaller death benefit without ongoing premiums.

Keeping Beneficiaries Informed: Discuss your policy with beneficiaries to make them aware of any critical details, such as the need to keep premiums up to date. This helps ensure the policy's intended benefits are realized and encourages everyone to stay proactive about the policy's status.

SAFEGUARDING YOUR POLICY FOR LONG-TERM SUCCESS

Avoiding a lapse is crucial to preserving both the cash value and death benefit of your life insurance policy. By setting up auto-payments, monitoring your cash value, and proactively managing any policy loans, you can protect your policy from lapses and the resulting financial setbacks.

In our next section, we'll explore how to assess whether life insurance is the right tool for your financial goals. With this foundation of understanding policy lapses and their consequences, you're better equipped to leverage your life insurance policy as a reliable asset for wealth building and income generation.

PART 6: IS LIFE INSURANCE A GOOD FIT FOR YOU?

21: LIFE INSURANCE AND YOUR FINANCIAL GOALS

THE ROLE OF LIFE INSURANCE IN YOUR FINANCIAL STRATEGY

L ife insurance can be a versatile financial tool, but it's not a one-size-fits-all solution. Deciding if life insurance aligns with your financial goals requires assessing your needs, priorities, and financial situation. In this chapter, we'll explore how to determine if life insurance is a suitable choice for your income goals, asset protection, and long-term planning.

KEY REASONS TO CONSIDER LIFE INSURANCE

Income Replacement for Dependents: One of the primary purposes of life insurance is to provide financial security to dependents in the event of an untimely death. If you have family members who rely on your income, life insurance can ensure they have financial support, covering essentials such as mortgage payments, educational expenses, and daily living costs.

Wealth-Building and Retirement Planning: Permanent life insurance policies, such as whole life or universal life, offer cash value accumulation that grows over time. This cash value can be leveraged to supplement retirement income or fund other investments, making it a useful tool for wealth-building. If retirement income and asset accumulation are among your financial priorities, permanent life insurance could be a valuable addition to your portfolio.

Tax Benefits and Estate Planning: Life insurance offers tax-free death benefits to beneficiaries, making it an efficient estate planning tool. If you're looking to leave an inheritance or reduce estate taxes, a life insurance policy can help preserve your wealth and reduce tax burdens for your heirs. Policies with cash value growth also provide tax-deferred savings, a benefit that may align with your tax-planning strategy.

Long-Term Savings for Future Goals: For those with long-term savings goals, such as funding college education or buying a home, certain life insurance policies can help build savings. Cash value accumulation allows you to save steadily over time, with funds accessible through loans or withdrawals when you need them.

UNDERSTANDING YOUR FINANCIAL NEEDS AND PRIORITIES

Assessing Income Needs and Financial Dependents: If your primary goal is to ensure financial stability for your family, calculate the amount of income they would need to maintain their lifestyle in your absence. This can include factoring in mortgage payments, educational costs, and day-to-day expenses. By evaluating these needs, you can determine whether life insurance is essential to your financial plan.

Identifying Asset Protection Goals: Life insurance can be used to protect assets, such as a business or significant real estate investments, that would otherwise be at risk in the event of your death. If maintaining ownership or covering debt obligations for these assets is a priority, life insurance can provide a safety net to protect your financial legacy.

Retirement and Supplemental Income: Consider your retirement income sources. If you're relying solely on retirement accounts, pensions, or Social Security, life insurance with cash value may serve as an additional retirement income source. Evaluate your retirement income needs to decide if a policy with cash value accumulation aligns with your goal of a comfortable retirement.

EVALUATING TYPES OF LIFE INSURANCE BASED ON YOUR GOALS

Term Life Insurance for Temporary Coverage: If you seek protection for a specific period, such as until a mortgage is paid off or until children are financially independent, term life insurance may be the best fit. Term policies are generally more affordable and provide substantial coverage for a set period, allowing you to meet short- or medium-term obligations.

Permanent Life Insurance for Long-Term Needs: If you're interested in building cash value or want lifelong coverage, consider permanent life insurance options like whole life or universal life. These policies can serve as a stable source of funds for retirement or wealth-building, but they come with higher premiums compared to term policies. Determine if the cash value growth potential aligns with your financial goals before committing to a permanent policy.

WEIGHING THE COSTS AND BENEFITS OF LIFE INSURANCE

Premium Affordability and Cash Flow: One of the most significant considerations is the affordability of premiums. Life insurance can be a considerable financial commitment, particularly for permanent policies. Review your cash flow to ensure that premium payments won't disrupt other financial priorities or cause strain on your budget.

Comparing Life Insurance with Other Investment Options: If you're considering life insurance primarily as an investment, compare the projected returns with other investment vehicles like retirement accounts, stocks, or real estate. While life insurance offers unique tax benefits and risk protection, other investments may offer higher returns, depending on your risk tolerance and financial goals.

SELF-ASSESSMENT: IS LIFE INSURANCE RIGHT FOR YOU?

Use this self-assessment to gauge whether life insurance aligns with your financial goals:

1. Do you have dependents who would need financial support in your absence?
2. Is accumulating tax-advantaged cash value a priority for your long-term financial planning?
3. Are you interested in using life insurance as a source of retirement income?
4. Do you have long-term debts or business obligations that would require coverage?
5. Is estate planning a key component of your financial strategy?

If you answered "yes" to most of these questions, life insurance could play a meaningful role in your financial strategy. If "no" was the answer to most questions, alternative savings and investment strategies might be more suitable.

NEXT STEPS: TAILORING LIFE INSURANCE TO FIT YOUR STRATEGY

Speaking with a Financial Advisor: A financial advisor can help you understand how life insurance integrates with your overall financial plan. Advisors can guide you through policy options, illustrate the cash value growth potential, and help you make an informed decision based on your financial objectives.

Reviewing Policy Illustrations and Projections: Life insurance policies include projections that estimate cash value growth and costs over time. Reviewing these illustrations can help you set realistic expectations and assess whether the policy aligns with your goals.

Periodic Policy Reviews: As your financial situation and goals evolve, review your policy periodically to ensure it remains aligned with your needs. Policy reviews allow you to adjust coverage, add riders, or modify payment plans to keep pace with changing financial priorities.

MAKING A CONFIDENT DECISION

Choosing to include life insurance in your financial strategy is a significant decision that should reflect your unique goals, risk tolerance, and long-term plans. Whether your focus is on income protection, retirement planning, or wealth building, understanding your objectives will guide you toward the best type of policy—or help you decide if life insurance isn't the right fit at this time.

In our next chapter, we'll discuss important self-assessment questions to better clarify your needs and help you decide on the next steps for selecting or enhancing your life insurance strategy. This will provide a foundation to confidently align your insurance choices with your overall financial objectives.

22: ASSESSING YOUR PERSONAL NEEDS

IDENTIFYING YOUR FINANCIAL GOALS

Understanding your personal financial needs is crucial when considering life insurance as part of your financial strategy. A thoughtful self-assessment can clarify your goals and guide you in making informed decisions about the type of coverage you may require.

In this chapter, we will explore essential self-assessment questions designed to help you evaluate your personal needs and determine whether life insurance is the right fit for you.

ASSESSING YOUR FINANCIAL RESPONSIBILITIES

Who relies on you financially?: Consider your dependents—spouse, children, elderly parents, or anyone else who depends on your income. Identifying these individuals will help you assess the level of financial support they may need in your absence.

What are your current financial obligations?: List your debts (mortgage, car loans, student loans) and regular expenses (utilities, groceries, education costs). Understanding these obligations can help you determine the amount of coverage necessary to secure your loved ones' financial stability.

Do you have any planned major life events?: Are there any upcoming life events, such as marriage, childbirth, or home purchase, that could impact your financial situation? Anticipating these changes can help you evaluate how your life insurance needs may evolve.

EVALUATING YOUR FINANCIAL GOALS

What is your primary reason for considering life insurance?: Are you primarily focused on income replacement, debt coverage, wealth accumulation, or estate planning? Defining your main goals will help you choose the right type of life insurance policy.

How do you envision your retirement?: Consider how you want to maintain your lifestyle in retirement. Will you need additional income streams, and could cash value from a life insurance policy play a role in your retirement planning?

Are you interested in leaving a financial legacy?: If leaving an inheritance for your beneficiaries is important to you, think about how life insurance can help you achieve that goal. Would you prefer a lump-sum payout, or are you considering options that provide long-term financial support?

UNDERSTANDING YOUR RISK TOLERANCE

How comfortable are you with financial risk?: Assess your risk tolerance regarding investments and financial products. If you prefer stability and guaranteed benefits, permanent life insurance may be a better fit than term insurance, which offers no cash value accumulation.

Are you prepared for potential policy costs?: Understand the premium payments associated with different types of life insurance. Are you comfortable with the ongoing costs, or do you prefer a more affordable, temporary solution like term life insurance?

EXPLORING YOUR INVESTMENT PREFERENCES

Do you have other investment vehicles in place?: Consider whether you have retirement accounts, savings, or other investments. If you're already investing elsewhere, determine if life insurance is necessary for your overall strategy or if other options would suffice.

What role do you want life insurance to play in your financial portfolio?: Decide if you want life insurance solely for protection or if you're looking for a combination of protection and investment growth. Understanding this will help you choose the appropriate type of life insurance.

PLANNING FOR THE FUTURE

How often do your financial needs change?: Evaluate whether your financial situation is stable or subject to frequent changes due to job status, family dynamics, or health. If your needs are likely to evolve, consider flexible life insurance options that can adapt to these changes.

Are you willing to reassess your life insurance needs regularly?: Life circumstances can shift, making it important to periodically review your policy and financial goals. Assess your willingness to engage in regular check-ins to ensure your life insurance remains aligned with your needs.

TAKING THE NEXT STEP

Completing this self-assessment can provide invaluable insight into your financial situation and needs regarding life insurance. By reflecting on these questions, you'll be better equipped to evaluate whether life insurance is a suitable option for your financial goals and which type of policy aligns best with your objectives.

In the final chapter, we'll guide you through the process of speaking with financial advisors and agents to ensure you make informed decisions based on your self-assessment insights. This will empower you to take actionable steps toward integrating life insurance into your overall financial strategy.

23: PLANNING NEXT STEPS

SPEAKING WITH ADVISORS AND PURCHASING A POLICY

Now that you have a clearer understanding of your personal financial needs and how life insurance can play a role in your financial strategy, it's time to take actionable steps towards securing the right policy. This chapter will guide you through the process of finding financial advisors, engaging in meaningful discussions, and making informed decisions when purchasing life insurance.

FINDING THE RIGHT FINANCIAL ADVISOR

Researching Financial Advisors: Start by researching qualified financial advisors who specialize in life insurance and financial planning. Look for professionals with credentials such as Certified Financial Planner (CFP), Chartered Life Underwriter (CLU), or other relevant designations. Online directories, professional organizations, and personal referrals can help you find reputable advisors in your area.

Evaluating Advisors: Before making a decision, evaluate potential advisors based on their experience, services offered, and approach to life insurance. Schedule initial consultations (often free) to discuss your needs and gauge their understanding of life insurance products. Ask about their commission structure and whether they offer fee-only services, which can provide more impartial advice.

PREPARING FOR YOUR MEETING

Organizing Your Financial Information: Before meeting with an advisor, gather your financial documents, including income statements, current insurance policies, debt information, and investment accounts. Having a clear picture of your finances will enable your advisor to provide tailored recommendations.

Defining Your Goals: Clearly articulate your financial goals and the role you envision for life insurance in your strategy. Consider the key points from your self-assessment, including your reasons for wanting life insurance and the amount of coverage you believe you need.

Creating a List of Questions: Prepare a list of questions to ask during your meeting. These may include:

- What type of life insurance do you recommend based on my needs?
- How much coverage do you suggest I consider?
- What are the costs associated with different policies?
- How do you get paid for your services?
- Can you explain the claims process and any additional benefits associated with the policies you recommend?

UNDERSTANDING POLICY OPTIONS

Types of Policies: As your advisor presents different policy options, pay attention to the features, benefits, and costs associated with each. This may include term life, whole life, and universal life insurance. Discuss how each policy aligns with your financial goals and preferences.

Comparing Quotes: Request quotes from multiple insurance providers. This will help you compare premiums, coverage options, and policy terms. Understanding the market can also provide leverage when negotiating with insurance companies.

Evaluating Riders: Discuss any optional riders that may enhance your coverage. Common riders include accelerated death benefits, disability waivers, and premium return options. Evaluate whether these add-ons align with your goals and budget.

MAKING YOUR PURCHASE

Finalizing Your Decision: After thoroughly discussing options with your advisor, take time to reflect on the information gathered. Ensure you are comfortable with your decision and that it aligns with your financial goals and values.

Completing the Application: Once you decide on a policy, you'll need to complete the application process. Be prepared to provide personal information, including health history, lifestyle habits, and financial details. The insurance company may also require a medical exam, depending on the coverage amount and policy type.

Understanding Policy Terms: After approval, review your policy documents carefully. Make sure you understand the coverage, terms, conditions, and any exclusions. Don't hesitate to ask your advisor or the insurance company any questions you have about the policy.

ONGOING REVIEW AND ADJUSTMENTS

Regular Check-ins: Once you've secured your policy, commit to regular check-ins with your advisor. Your financial needs and goals may change over time, and it's essential to reassess your coverage to ensure it remains appropriate.

Updating Your Policy: Be proactive in updating your policy as significant life events occur, such as marriage, the birth of children, or changes in employment. These milestones may require adjustments to your coverage to adequately protect your loved ones.

TAKING CONTROL OF YOUR FINANCIAL FUTURE

Purchasing life insurance is a crucial step in your financial journey. By speaking with knowledgeable advisors, understanding your options, and making informed decisions, you'll be better equipped to secure the right coverage for your needs. This proactive approach will help you take control of your financial future, ensuring that you and your loved ones are protected for years to come.

CONCLUSION

YOUR NEXT STEPS TO FINANCIAL GROWTH AND SECURITY

C ongratulations on reaching the end of *Life Insurance Investing 101: Simple Strategies for Growing Wealth with Life Insurance.* The end of this book is not the conclusion of your journey in deepening your knowledge on this subject; by taking action and engaging in further study, you will gain knowledge, skills, and experience as you continue along your path.

As we've learned the intricacies of using life insurance as a wealth-building tool, it's clear that this often-underestimated asset holds tremendous potential for generating income and securing your financial future.

Throughout the book, we have explored various strategies for maximizing your policy's cash value, understanding dividends, and leveraging your life insurance for loans and investments.

You now have the knowledge to navigate the complexities of life insurance with confidence, enabling you to make informed decisions that align with your unique financial goals. Whether you choose to access your cash value, reinvest dividends, or use your policy as collateral, each option can enhance your overall financial strategy.

The key to successfully using this wealth-building strategy lies not only in understanding the mechanics of life insurance but also in being proactive and strategic about how you utilize it.

As you move forward, continue to assess your financial needs and goals regularly. Life insurance is not just a safety net; it's a versatile financial tool that can help you create additional income streams and build wealth over time. With the insights and strategies outlined in this book, you are well-equipped to unlock the full potential of your life insurance policy.

Take charge of your financial future today—start implementing these strategies and watch as your life insurance transforms into a powerful asset.

Thank you for investing time in this journey to learn more about how life insurance can support your financial goals. Here's to taking control of your financial future and making life insurance work for you.

ABOUT THE AUTHOR

Usiere Uko

Usiere Uko is a Consultant, ILO Certified Trainer, and Business & Finance Author focused on financial independence and entrepreneurship. A former oil and gas engineer turned entrepreneur, he helps individuals and business owners build sustainable income, make smarter financial decisions, and grow resilient businesses.

He is a certified Business Development Service Provider (BDSP) and an ILO-certified trainer in SIYB and WIDB, and currently serves as Lead Consultant at Sageway Consulting and Training Coordinator at The Citadel Business Academy.

Usiere writes in a friendly and practical style, making complex financial and business ideas simple, clear, and actionable for everyday readers and entrepreneurs. He is based in Lagos, Nigeria.

BOOKS IN THIS SERIES

ALTERNATIVE INCOME & PASSIVE CASH FLOW

Annuities Investing 101: A Beginner's Guide To Guaranteed Income For Life

Life Insurance Investing 101: Simple Strategies For Growing Wealth With Life Insurance

Peer-To-Peer Lending Investing 101: Simple Strategies For Earning Passive Income Through Lending

Forex Investing 101: Simple Strategies For Earning From Currency Markets Without Active Trading

BOOKS BY THIS AUTHOR

Practical Steps To Financial Freedom And Independence: Money Management Skills For Beginners

101 Common Money Mistakes To Avoid: And How To Fix Them. Book 1: Expenses. Money Management, Making Your Budget Work

Financial Independence For Employees: Making Your Job A Stepping Stone To Exiting The Rat Race And Living Your Dreams

Managing Your Money Post Covid: Financial Management Skills For An Era Of High Inflation And Market Disruption

Retire On Your Own Terms: A Simple Guide To Financially Literate Retirement Planning

Your Ultimate Money Makeover: Manage Your Money Better, Take Control Of Your Finances And

Your Life

Teaching Kids Money 101: Simple Parenting Strategies For Raising Financially Literate Kids From Toddler To Teen Years And Beyond

Uncle Ben's Money Lessons: Book I: Do You Want To Work For Money? A Vacation Story With An Adventure Into The World Of Money

Gold Trading 101: The Beginner's Guide To Unlocking The Potential Of Precious Metals

Forex Trading 101: A Beginner's Guide And Strategies To Profitable Currency Trading

A Beginner's Guide To The Nigerian Money Market: Simple Steps To Saving For Investing And Building Wealth In Nigeria

Your Debt-Free Journey: A Roadmap To Freedom From Bad Debt And Achieving Financial Independence

Money Matters Manual And Activity Book: Financial Literacy Beginner's Guide And Puzzles

For Smart Kids And Adults

How To Avoid Living Under Financial Pressure: A Simple Guide To Getting Back Control Of Your Finances, Repaying Bad Debts And Growing Your Income

www.ingramcontent.com/pod-product-compliance
Lightning Source LLC
Chambersburg PA
CBHW071514220526
45472CB00003B/1029